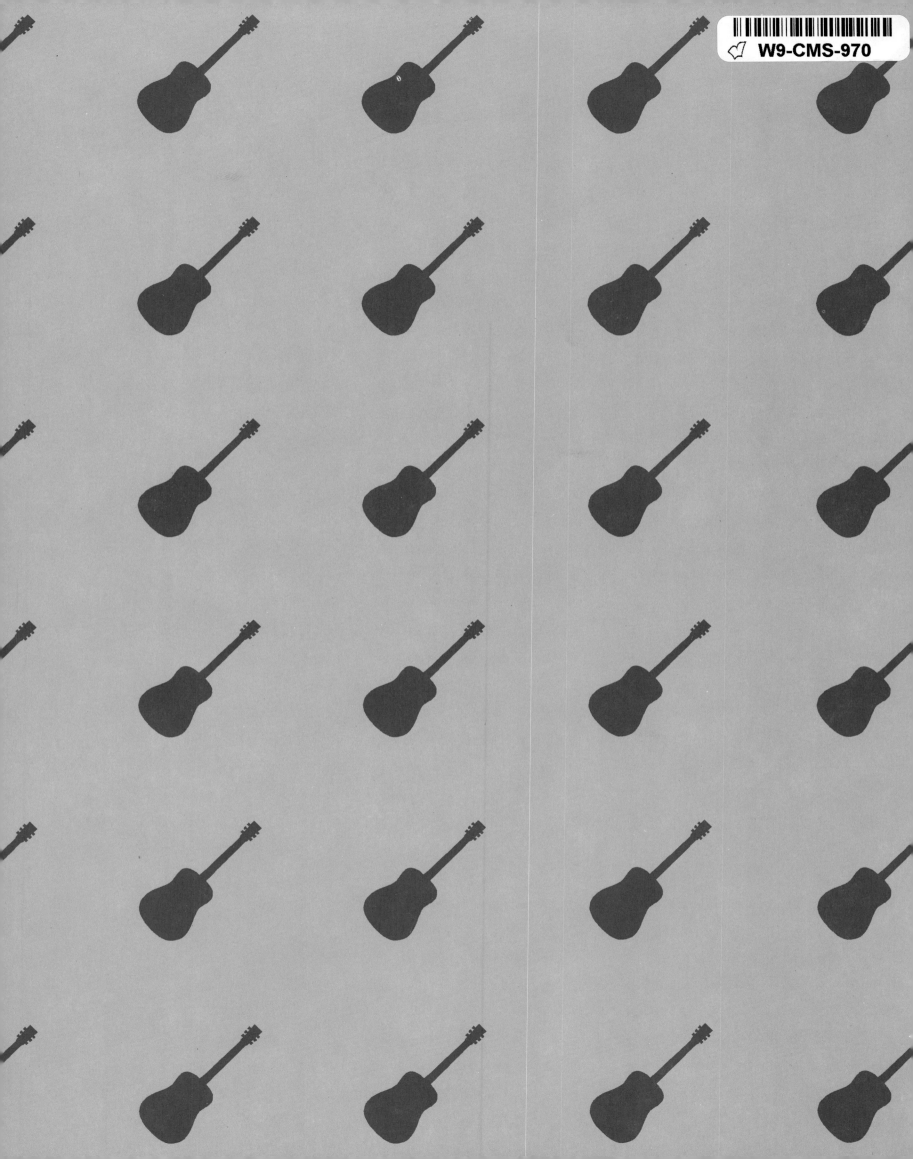

COUNTRY
MUSIC STARS

THE LEGENDS
AND THE NEW BREED

AUTHORS
Michael McCall
Dave Hoekstra
Janet Williams

PUBLICATIONS INTERNATIONAL, LTD.

CONTRIBUTING WRITERS

MICHAEL McCALL is a Nashville-based country music and entertainment writer whose credits include a biography of Garth Brooks and articles in *US* and *Billboard*. He served as music critic and feature writer for the *Nashville Banner* for seven years, and currently is a columnist for the *Nashville Scene*.

DAVE HOEKSTRA is the country music writer of the Chicago *Sun-Times*, where his features and columns on country, entertainment, and popular culture have appeared since 1981. As contributing editor to *Chicago Magazine* he provided critical commentary and stories on rock, jazz, and blues music and nightlife.

JANET WILLIAMS, a Nashville resident, has closely followed the country music scene by interviewing performers and writing features in her role as associate editor of *Close Up*, the magazine of the Country Music Association. Previously, she served as an associate producer of USA Network's *Night Flight*.

Special acknowledgment to Don Roy, Ronnie Pugh of the Country Music Foundation, and Otto Kitsinger for their contributions to this book.

Louis Weber, C.E.O.
Publications International, Ltd.
7373 North Cicero Avenue
Lincolnwood, Illinois 60646

Permission is never granted for commercial purposes.

Manufactured in USA

8 7 6 5 4 3 2 1

ISBN 1-56173-697-X

CONTENTS

CONTENTS

An extraordinary galaxy of luminaries has shaped the world of country music. The participants have been unassuming, pretentious, profane, sweetly likeable, predictable, and unpredictable. Like summer stars and winter snowflakes, no two country musicians are alike.

Country is indeed the correct label for these artists, because their voices call out from every corner of America—from the Texas panhandle to the Tennessee River, from a bar in Bakersfield, California, to a New York honky-tonk. Country music is a glorious hybrid of American musical influences.

Sid Harkreader, vaudeville partner of seminal country star Uncle Dave Macon in the early 1920s, has been cited as the first fiddler to perform on Nashville's WSM radio.

Country musicians inherited their ragged but right independence from descendants in rural folk music. Free of any commercial obligation, rural folk artists were adventurous and untamed. Texas fiddle player A.C. "Eck" Robertson is regarded as being the first to bring rural folk into a country landscape with his 1922 recording of "Sallie Gooden." Robertson's playing was fluid and fierce; a Texas comet burning across tight traditional strings. The Texan was also one of the first musicians to wear full western regalia while performing.

But the early years of country music were amazingly fertile, and Eck Robertson was not the only game in town. At the same time as Robertson's success, another Texan, Vernon Dalhart, was determined to take the rural sound uptown. Dalhart had moved to New York City and was singing country music in churches and vaudeville houses. Some observers called Dalhart's style "Tin Pan Alley Country."

The simultaneous yet quite different careers of Robertson and Dalhart established a country-music truth that remains valid today: For every action there is a reaction. Eck Robertson was a hick, Vernon Dalhart was slick. Country music has been a music of response. One approach inspires another, and so it was that the success of Robertson and Dalhart helped inspire still another sort of country that came to be known as hillbilly music.

Above: *College-educated Tex Ritter epitomized the ideal of the soft-spoken and principled western hero.* Far right: *Eddy Arnold brought smooth crooning to country in the 1940s.*

Popular music was riding a wave of nostalgia in the mid-1920s. The ragtime of the Gay Nineties was enjoying a revival. Country musicians knew most of those songs because in the rural South they probably never went out of style. In 1925 Okeh Records executive Ralph Peer recorded a North Carolina string band in New York City. The musicians described themselves as hillbillies

in the big city. When Peer named the group the Hill Billies, country music picked up its first mass-culture identity.

The most significant performer of the hillbilly period was Jimmie Rodgers. It was in 1925 that Rodgers quit his job as a railroad worker and devoted himself to music full-time. By 1927, he was being recorded by Peer in the legendary Bristol, Tennessee sessions.

Because Rodgers's roots were in Mississippi, he had an advantage over his Texas counterparts: he had heard rural blues on the radio and had worked with blacks on the railroad. By mixing the simple forcefulness of field blues with hillbilly music, Rodgers became country music's first star.

Jimmie Rodgers is the jumping off point for this book. Keep his rural blue yodel in the back of your mind as you trace the development of country music via the book's performer profiles. You will see that no form of popular music has endured as much change as country music.

At one time or another country music has been about hillbillies, rebels, Nashville sophisticates, outlaws, real cowboys, rhinestone cowboys, urban cowboys, and—as country music strides into the nineties—suburban cowboys.

Country music's evolution has not always been easy. Many performers have

Far left: Guitar virtuoso Chet Atkins has made prolific contributions to the evolution of country music as a musician, producer, and executive. Above: Bill Monroe created the musical style he dubbed "bluegrass." Below: The Grand Ole Opry, 1951, with Chet Atkins, Mother Maybelle Carter, and daughters June, Anita, and Helen Carter.

had to struggle to break preconceived notions about what country music should be. When the hillbilly sound was superseded by honky-tonk in the 1940s, some people were shocked by honky-tonk's introduction of electric guitars, piano, and drums. Lyrics reflected the new, bawdy sound, and many songs were clearly addressed to the culturally and socially disenfranchised. Finally, vast numbers of Americans had a "voice."

Country music's evolution continued, and the infectious din of honky-tonk was drowned out by the melodramatic slickness of The Nashville Sound. Smooth, calculated, swelling with lush string arrangements, The Nashville Sound defined country music for years—at least until the outlaw movement roared up as a rebellious response.

Today, country music is an amalgam of the best of what has come before, combined with a contemporary spin that makes the music as fresh and as popular as it has ever been.

Above: *The Opry marches on: Johnny Cash puts over a song during a July 1972 Opry appearance. Far right: Nova Scotia native Hank Snow is a brilliant guitar player and a versatile singer who patterned his early vocal style on that of Jimmie Rodgers.*

Country Music Stars examines the changing history of country music through artist profiles arranged in four distinct chronological sections. "Roots: The 1920s and 1930s" looks at the evolution of country music during its seminal years. "Classics: The 1940s and 1950s" covers the war years and immediate postwar era—a period of great liveliness and innovation in country music. "The Next Generation: The 1960s and 1970s" explores the period of commercial explosion that brought country music to a receptive mainstream audience. The book's final section, "The New Breed: The 1980s and 1990s" looks at the hot country artists of today, who have propelled country music to unparalleled popularity and record-chart dominance.

Artist profiles in every section give useful biographical information and, more importantly, insights into each performer's musical strengths and significance. A handy "fact box" that follows each profile encapsulates the star's life and career.

If there is one characteristic that links the country music stars of all eras, it is integrity. From Jimmie Rodgers to Garth Brooks, Patsy Montana to Reba McEntire, country musicians have written and performed

Following a stint in San Quentin, Merle Haggard pulled himself back from the brink in the 1960s and became one of the best songwriters and most uncompromising vocalists in country music.

truthful songs that come from the heart.

Country performers are fortunate to have been brought up with the humble belief that anyone can make music in any environment—on the front porch, in the family room, in a rural church or in a honky-tonk, and yes,

Left: *The profound success of Dolly Parton in country music, pop, television, and movies helped introduce a mass audience to the country style in the 1970s and '80s. Despite the glitz and glamour of her persona, Parton is as purely "country" as they come.*

Above: *By mixing country passion with edgy elements of rock 'n' roll, Steve Earle became a highly visible proponent of country's "neo-traditionalist" movement in the mid-'80s. His simultaneous interest in country's past and future is shared by many of his contemporaries.*

maybe someday in a fancy studio in Nashville. The legends examined in the following pages—Roy Acuff, Johnny Cash, Patsy Cline, Merle Haggard, George Jones, Ernest Tubb, Hank Williams—all became country artists as an expression of their rural tradition. But today's country musicians come from a more sophisticated American culture that permits them the freedom to choose whichever musical course they wish. And they are a generation who chose country music. That is the ultimate tribute.

The twinkle of country music stars has never been so bright.

Fiddlin' John Carson is considered to be the first country music soloist to perform live on the radio. He made his broadcast debut in 1922.

Onetime Broadway performer Vernon Dalhart was a trained vocalist who specialized in light opera. He recorded his first country song in 1924.

As the 1920s began, several musicians across the southern portion of the United States were making decent livings at civic gatherings and fiddle contests performing old-style folk songs and rustic versions of Tin Pan Alley hits. In Texas, for example, fiddler Eck Robertson and his guitar-strumming friend Henry Gilliland were having a fine time performing at political functions and in theaters during the showing of silent films. The two were willing to travel to find new audiences, and in the summer of 1922 they decided to journey to a Civil War reunion in Virginia, figuring they could pay for the trip with money picked up from the huge crowds expected to attend.

The Virginia trip went so well that the two enterprising instrumentalists decided to go on to New York and look into the new business of making phonograph recordings. When they showed up at the offices of Victor Records, Robertson was dressed as an Old West cowboy and Gilliland wore a Confederate uniform. The Victor executives reportedly were amused by these bold yokels and took them into the studio.

Robertson and Gilliland didn't intend to enter into history or into a long-running debate about the origin of the first country music recordings. However, the two cut several songs, including Robertson's solo rendition of the fiddle tune "Sallie Gooden." Many music historians have referred to these Victor sessions as the first country music recordings and to "Sallie Gooden" as country's first hit.

There were other country-music pioneers. Fiddlin' John Carson was a popular radio performer on WSB in Atlanta, and Okeh Records executive Ralph Peer recorded Carson's "Little Old Log Cabin in the Lane" in June of 1923. George Banman Grayson and Henry Whitter were a duo who, like Robertson and Gilliland, traveled to New York without an invitation but ended up recording several songs now considered country music standards, including "Handsome Molly" and "Little Maggie."

No one referred to these as country songs at the time. The genre of mountain tunes and folk blues of Southern rural whites gained its first name when Ralph Peer asked a string band he had just recorded what they wanted to be called. "Call us anything you want," answered a band member. "We're just a bunch of hillbillies from Virginia and North Carolina." Peer dubbed them the Hill Billies, and the phrase was soon transformed into a one-word adjective, as in hillbilly music, and used to describe this developing genre of simple songs.

By 1924, country music had its first million seller, "The Prisoner's Song" by Vernon Dalhart, a Broadway performer who had appeared in a Gilbert & Sullivan production before seeing a career opportunity in performing for the growing rural record market. The growth had been pushed along by the increasing influence of radio, which gave the rural population a chance to hear and enjoy music that once had been accessible only to urban audiences.

Radio station WBAP in Fort Worth fueled the growing Southern folk music boom in early 1923 by presenting a barn-dance program that inspired a great listener response. Chicago's WLS followed with the *National Barn*

Dance and a few years later WSM in Nashville began its own variety barn dance hour that would later turn into a three-hour program known as the *Grand Ole Opry*. There, a jovial banjo picker named Uncle Dave Macon and a black harmonica player, DeFord Bailey, built an audience that expanded further once Roy Acuff came along in the 1930s to become the Opry's first superstar.

At first, country music didn't sell quite as well as opera and classical or the popular Tin Pan Alley hits, but it was cheap to produce and it helped the young recording firms reach a previously untapped audience. Then Ralph Peer stumbled upon country music's first superstar when he recorded Jimmie Rodgers in Bristol, Tennessee, while on a July 1927 recording trek through the Southeast. The same day, Peer also cut the first records of the Carter Family, thereby launching two of country music's most significant acts within hours of each other.

Far left: *The flamboyant Uncle Dave Macon was the Grand Ole Opry's first star.* Above: *DeFord Bailey, a gifted harmonica player, was the Opry's most popular performer in the late 1920s.* Below: *Roy Acuff (center) and the Crazy Tennesseans in 1939. With Acuff are (from left) Pete Kirby, Jess Easterday, Rachel Veach, and Lonnie "Pap" Wilson.*

Peer's two discoveries represented the diversity that would remain a hallmark of country music through the decades. Rodgers was a rambling, gambling man who liked to drink, carouse, and live life to the fullest. He incorporated the blues into his music and experimented with new musical ideas. The Carters, on the other hand, were devoutly religious and domestic people who preferred songs about family, faith, and their native region. They stuck closely to the traditional musical styles of their home throughout their careers.

By the late 1930s, the cinematic image of the romantic, rugged cowboy had become a prominent aspect of American popular culture, and movie star Gene Autry was achieving record sales comparable to those of Bing Crosby and other mainstream stars. As the era drew to a close and America became increasingly industrialized, people from coast to coast were singing simple, heartfelt songs inspired by the music that originated in the South and the West. They were even beginning to call this hillbilly style by a new, more respectable name: country and western music.

Left: *The Jimmie Rodgers Entertainers, 1927; the leader's bespectacled look belies the rambling lifestyle that was at the core of much of his music.* Opposite: *Publicity photos often showed Rodgers wearing a straw boater, but for this shot he chose a dapper bowler.*

Jimmie Rodgers started the train rolling. Known as the father of commercial country music, he was the first entertainer to prove that a blended hodgepodge of Southern musical styles could attract listeners across America. He was the first country music star, selling an estimated 20 million copies of recordings made in the last six years of his short life.

Musically, Rodgers borrowed sounds from African-American blues and jazz and combined them with mountain music to create a style uniquely his own. He also perpetuated many of country music's primary themes: He sang about drinking and rambling,

lasting love and homesickness, mother and country, cowboys and prairies, loose women and one-night stands. He wrote overtly sentimental songs and tunes with bawdy double entendres.

Rodgers was born on September 8, 1897, in Last Gap, Mississippi. His father worked as a foreman for the Mobile & Ohio Railroad. His mother had been infirm for most of her adult life, dying of tuberculosis when her youngest son was seven years old.

At age 14, Rodgers landed a laborious job in the railroad yard as a water carrier. Many of Rodgers's coworkers were blacks who sang spirituals and old slave songs; the

boy became fascinated by those who could make music with the guitar, banjo, ukelele, mandolin, and other instruments.

Throughout his life, Rodgers worked a variety of jobs for the railroads, including stints as a flagman and as a baggage master. He also worked as a brakeman, a premier job on the railroad line, which accounted for his nickname "the Singing Brakeman." While riding the trains, he began mimicking the long, lonesome wail of a train whistle, transforming it into a plaintive kind of yodel that would become his frequently imitated trademark.

Though Rodgers would later romanticize his employment with the railroads, he was probably more interested in pursuing a career as a performer than riding the rails. While still a teenager, he ran away from home to join a medicine show. An early marriage disintegrated because, according to his first wife, he couldn't make a decent living "plunking on some old banjo or guitar."

In April 1920, he married second wife Carrie Williamson, the seventh daughter of a preacher. Carrie's strict, refined upbringing was the opposite of her husband's rough, rowdy way of life. The couple lived in poverty, and their second child died in infancy. Ominously, Rodgers began to struggle with the heavy coughs and

Jimmie Rodgers loved automobiles, the faster the better, and he collected several of them shortly after making the climb from itinerant musician to nationally known singing star.

colds that had beset his mother. He suffered a hemorrhage in 1925 and spent three months in the hospital, where he was diagnosed with tuberculosis and advised to give up the hard-working railroad life.

To make money, Rodgers performed as a minstrel singer in blackface on the street corners of Meridian. He was hired by a medicine show that took him to Tennessee and Kentucky, and for two years after that he worked at a variety of jobs while traveling with

Carrie and his daughter, Anita, through Florida, Arizona, Texas, and North Carolina.

In 1927, he formed the Jimmie Rodgers Entertainers in Asheville, North Carolina. He read a newspaper account of auditions being held by Victor Records executive Ralph Peer in Bristol, Tennessee, and convinced his three partners to audition with him.

However, once in Bristol, the group dissolved and his partners auditioned as a trio. Rodgers

convinced Peer to give him a shot as a solo artist. One of his two songs, "Soldier's Sweetheart," gained enough radio play to persuade Rodgers to move his family to Washington, D.C., near RCA Victor's New Jersey recording center.

His first session in Camden, New Jersey, included "Blue Yodel No. 1," also known as "T for Texas," the song that established Rodgers as a major American recording star. Shortly, he was

"The Yodeling Cowboy" was one of many nicknames Rodgers acquired during his brief but very successful career. Others included "The Singing Brakeman" and "The Blue Yodeler."

while on tour. Discovering that most of his wealth had been spent on extravagances and health care, he set up a prolonged recording session with Victor Records in New York.

He left Texas in May 1933 to cut 24 songs with Peer in New York, perhaps understanding the need to add to his legacy as quickly as possible. His disease had progressed to a point where he had to rest on a cot between songs, and his last session took place on May 20. He spent his remaining days confined to his room in the Taft Hotel, and on the morning of May 26, 1933, the hotel maid found him unconscious and hemorrhaging. Rodgers died that day, less than six years after his initial recording.

In 1961, Jimmie Rodgers joined Hank Williams and Fred Rose as the first inductees into the Country Music Hall of Fame.

earning $2,000 a month in record royalties plus touring fees from the vaudeville circuit, which took him almost instantaneously from poverty to fame and affluence.

By 1930, Rodgers's jaunty country blues and sentimental songs put him at the forefront of American musical celebrities. He took enormous pleasure from his fame, living fast and on-the-move, and indulging his love for fast cars by collecting several of his own. He recorded with Louis Armstrong in Hollywood, socialized with film stars Stan Laurel and Oliver Hardy, and joined Will Rogers on a tour of the South to raise money for dustbowl victims.

He also was suffering increasingly debilitating bouts of tuberculosis. In 1931, at the height of his fame, he recorded "T.B. Blues," which stated with gutsy directness: "I've been fighting like a lion, looks like I'm going to lose, 'cause there ain't nobody ever whipped the T.B. blues."

Rodgers spent time in a Houston hospital in 1933, after collapsing

> **JIMMIE RODGERS**
> **Real name:** James Charles Rodgers
> **Born:** September 8, 1897; Last Gap, Mississippi
> **Died:** May 26, 1933; New York, New York
> **First hit:** "Blue Yodel No. 1 (T for Texas)" (1928)
> **Other notable hits:** "In the Jailhouse Now" (1928), "Waiting for a Train" (1929), "My Rough and Rowdy Ways" (1929), "Anniversary Blue Yodel (Blue Yodel No. 7)" (1929), "Pistol Packin' Papa" (1930), "Blue Yodel No. 8 (Muleskinner Blues)" (1930)
> **Awards and achievements:** Country Music Hall of Fame (1961); Honored by Rock 'n' Roll Hall of Fame (1986)

THE CARTER FAMILY

The Carter family dressed in their Sunday finest for this publicity shot from the 1920s. Maybelle stands to the left, next to A. P. and cousin Sara. Traditional to their core, the Carters created music that resonates with simple honesty. Interestingly, the Carters were discovered by Victor Records executive Ralph Peer on the same day Peer discovered Jimmie Rodgers.

The Carter Family became country music's first commercially successful "traditional" act. They performed songs that were as old as the communities in the Clinch Mountain area where Alvin, Sara, and Maybelle Carter had been raised. Their folksy, string-band sound helped them to become one of America's most popular singing groups as well as one of country music's most endearing and enduring recording acts.

Alvin Pleasant "A. P." Carter, the oldest member, was born in April 1891 in a log cabin in the mountains near Maces Spring, Virginia. He married Sara Dougherty, a resident of Copper Creek, located on the other side of Clinch Mountain. Sara's younger cousin, Maybelle Addington, married A.P.'s brother Ezra shortly after her 16th birthday in 1925.

All three shared a love for music, and they began performing together on front porches and in living rooms around Maces Spring. Sara played the autoharp and sang in a husky, compellingly beautiful voice. Maybelle played guitar in an accomplished two-finger style, her

A. P. and Sara Carter (at left) were divorced when this photo was taken in the 1950s. The couple's daughter, Janette, stands in the center beside Kathleen and A. L. Phipps, who recorded as the Carter-influenced Phipps Family.

thumb providing the melody on the bass strings while her fingers strummed the rhythm on the tenor strings. A.P. sang bass and also collected songs, hunting down traditional folk tunes in old hymnals, sheet music, and by transcribing lyrics from informants and fans. A.P. did not merely disseminate traditional rural music—he also preserved it.

The Carter Family's well-blended talents earned them invitations to perform at schoolhouses, church picnics, and other community gatherings. In 1927, Victor Records executive Ralph Peer traveled to their area seeking local talent. On August 1, Peer recorded the Carter Family's first songs on the same day he discovered and recorded Jimmie Rodgers.

At Victor's encouragement, the Carters traveled to Camden, New Jersey, for a recording session that resulted in "Wildwood Flower" and "Keep on the Sunny Side," two of their best-known hits. Their songs became well-known throughout the South, but the austere, simple-living Carters didn't earn the fortunes acquired by Rodgers. The family worked the Carter farm and maintained other jobs, traveling only sporadically to nearby states until 1938, when they moved to Del Rio, Texas. There, they performed regularly on Mexican border station XERA, which had a 50,000-watt signal that reached across the West, Midwest, and South.

Although A.P. and Sara separated in 1933 and divorced in 1938,

the trio continued to record and perform. In the group's later years, Sara's daughter, Janette, and Maybelle's daughters, Helen, June, and Anita, joined the group. In 1943, A.P. and Sara retired from music, while Maybelle continued to perform with her daughters as Mother Maybelle and the Carter Sisters.

The Carter Family sang about an America of simple, rural values and agricultural traditions that had virtually disappeared by the time of their success, giving their music a hint of melancholy that pervades country music even today.

THE CARTER FAMILY

Real names: Alvin Pleasant Carter; Sara Dougherty Carter; Maybelle Addington Carter

Born: (Alvin) April 15, 1891; Maces Spring, Virginia

(Sara) July 21, 1898; Wise County, Virginia

(Maybelle) May 10, 1909; Nickelsville, Virginia

Died: (Alvin) November 7, 1960; Maces Spring, Virginia

(Sara) January 8, 1979; Lodi, California

(Maybelle) October 23, 1978; Madison, Tennessee

First hit: "Wildwood Flower" (1928)

Other notable hits: "Keep on the Sunny Side" (1928), "Gold Watch and Chain," "Thinking Tonight of My Blue Eyes," "The Worried Man Blues," "Will the Circle Be Unbroken," "Hello Stranger." The same songs were recorded often; dates of the hit versions are difficult to establish.

Awards and achievements: Country Music Hall of Fame (1970); A. P. Carter Highway designated in Virginia

THE DELMORE BROTHERS

The Delmore Brothers combined the rural gospel harmonies of the Carter Family with the rustic blues instrumentation of Jimmie Rodgers. The duo attained only limited success in their time, but their harmonies, songwriting, and delicately swinging music influenced scores of musicians.

Growing up in Alabama's rural Limestone County, Alton Delmore (born Christmas Day, 1908) became intrigued with the four-part harmonies that his uncle, Will Williams, taught him. Rabon Delmore (born December 3, 1916) was nine years old when he started joining his elder brother in local performances.

In October 1931, the duo recorded their first songs with Columbia Records. The following year, they joined the Grand Ole Opry, becoming one of the show's first vocal acts. In 1938, the Delmores hired Roy Acuff and his band as their opening act, giving the future country legend his first big break.

The Delmores left the Opry in 1938, going on to host a radio show in Birmingham and to join the Boone County Jamboree in Cincinnati. There they started a side project with Merle Travis and Grandpa Jones known as the Brown's Ferry Four, a popular gospel harmony group.

In 1946, the brothers hired harmonica player Wayne Raney, who led them toward a new sound incorporating boogie rhythms. The duo recorded their most famous song, "Blues Stay Away From Me," with Raney.

In 1950, Alton suffered a minor heart attack and retired from

Rabon (left) and Alton Delmore were among the stars who helped lead the Grand Ole Opry toward an emphasis on vocal performers. The Delmores' high harmonies and blues-based music influenced two generations of country performers.

music; he passed away in 1964. Rabon developed lung cancer and died in 1952. Alton's autobiography, *Truth is Stranger than Publicity*, was published posthumously by the Country Music Foundation.

Alton Delmore (seated) wrote more than a thousand songs, including the standards "Blues Stay Away From Me" and "Brown's Ferry Blues." He aspired to be a novelist and wrote an autobiography, Truth is Stranger than Publicity.

THE DELMORE BROTHERS

Real names: Alton Delmore; Rabon Delmore

Born: (Alton) December 25, 1908; Elkmont, Alabama
(Rabon) December 3, 1916; Elkmont, Alabama

Died: (Alton) June 8, 1964; Nashville, Tennessee
(Rabon) December 4, 1952; Athens, Alabama

First hit: "Brown's Ferry Blues" (1933)

Other notable hits: "I've Got the Big River Blues" (1934), "Beautiful Brown Eyes" (1935), "Midnight Special" (1946), "Hillbilly Boogie" (1947), "Freight Train Boogie" (1947), "Blues Stay Away From Me" (1950)

Awards and achievements: Seminal "brother duet" act; popularized country-music use of blues, boogie, and ragtime influences; Grand Ole Opry members, 1932-38

Patsy Montana was the first solo female country music star, and her 1935 hit, "I Wanna Be a Cowboy's Sweetheart," was the first million-selling record by a woman.

Montana was born Ruby Blevins in 1912 near Hot Springs, Arkansas. (She later added an "e" to her first name, spelling it "Rubye.") She grew up as the only female in a family with ten boys, so she learned independence early.

Montana taught herself to sing, yodel, and play guitar and fiddle while a youngster. She polished her violin skills at the University of the West (now UCLA) but decided she would rather be involved in western music. She eventually formed a female trio known as the Montana Cowgirls, taking the group's name from Monty Montana, a world-champion roper and cowboy. Another woman in the group was known as Ruthie, which was close in pronunciation to Rubye. So singer Stuart Hamblen changed Rubye's name to Patsy Montana while introducing the trio on a radio show.

In 1933, Montana joined the Prairie Ramblers, a male quartet who performed on WLS *National Barn Dance* in Chicago. Montana landed her famous million-selling hit two years later, and she and the Prairie Ramblers remained major touring and recording stars until 1949. She also appeared in a couple of western-movie serials with Gene Autry.

Montana moved to California in the mid-1950s with husband Paul Rose. She continues to perform sporadically in the United States and Europe.

Patsy Montana's 1935 hit, "I Wanna Be a Cowboy's Sweetheart," made her yodel one of the most famous in America.

PATSY MONTANA
Real name: Ruby Blevins
Born: October 30, 1912; Hot Springs, Arkansas
First hit: "I Wanna Be a Cowboy's Sweetheart" (1935)
Other notable hits: "Sweetheart of the Saddle" (1936), "I Want to Be a Cowboy's Sweetheart No. 2 (I've Found My Cowboy Sweetheart)" (1937), "There's a Ranch in the Sky" (1937), "Singing in the Saddle" (1939), "Shy Little Ann from Cheyenne" (1940)
Awards and achievements: "I Wanna Be a Cowboy's Sweetheart": first million-selling record by a woman

More recently, she has continued to perform for her fans.

ROY ACUFF

Left: *Roy Acuff began performing on Knoxville radio station WNOX in 1933, five years before he made his debut on the Grand Ole Opry.* Opposite: *Not simply an accomplished entertainer, Acuff fashioned himself into a powerhouse of Nashville music publishing.*

The most important day in the career of Roy Acuff was February 19, 1938. He was 34 years old and thin, solemn, and determined. He was also more nervous than he'd ever been in his life. He was making his debut at the Grand Ole Opry that evening. In previous years, he had auditioned several times, always failing to gain an invitation to go on the show. But he and his band, the Crazy Tennesseans, had made a name for themselves on a Knoxville radio station, finally earning him a chance.

He forgot the words of his opening gospel number and made several mistakes on the fiddle. So he changed plans by telling the band to play "The Great Speckled Bird," a traditional hymn that he sang and didn't have to play. Acuff performed it with complete conviction, letting his unadorned, plaintive voice soar with intensity. The crowd roared its approval.

Acuff returned to Knoxville. Two weeks later, he received a letter inviting him to become an Opry regular. WSM, which broadcasts the live Opry show, had been inundated with fan mail following his performance.

Acuff soon proved just as important to the Opry as it was to him. Opry management encouraged him to change the name of his band from the Crazy Tennesseans to the Smoky Mountain Boys, then made Acuff the core of a promotional blitz designed to raise the Opry's ability to sell tickets during package concerts across America. The campaign worked: The Opry became the premier radio program in the South, and Acuff became one of country music's biggest attractions in the early 1940s.

The singer was born on September 15, 1903, in Maynardville in eastern Tennessee. His father, Neill Acuff, was a missionary Baptist preacher and

lawyer who played the fiddle. As a youngster, Acuff excelled at sports, earning 13 athletic letters in high school. He also acted in theatrical productions at school.

His original ambition was to become a professional baseball player. He earned an invitation to try out for the New York Yankees, but prior to the big-league audition he suffered a severe sunstroke during a semi-pro game on July 7, 1929. The sunstroke hit him again a week later, then once more three months after that. The fourth one hit during a game of golf, and Ray was forced to end his sports career and spend much of his time indoors regaining his strength.

Acuff went to work as a callboy in railroad yards, where he learned to mimic the blast of the train whistle. This strengthened his voice and provided him with a vocal technique that would serve him well in the years ahead. He also started to pursue music with a vengeance, and soon was hired to go on tour with a neighbor who headed a medicine show. By 1933, he had formed a band and gained a regular job as a live performer with a Knoxville radio station.

Roy Acuff and the Crazy Tennesseans made their first recordings for the American Record Corporation in 1936. "The Great Speckled Bird" was recorded at that time, as was "The Wabash Cannon Ball," a Carter Family

Acuff on the Grand Ole Opry, an institution he helped establish and came to represent as its most famous star. He's flanked here by longtime band members Lonnie "Pap" Wilson (left) and Beecher "Pete" Kirby.

"Pap" Wilson on guitar.

By 1942, Acuff was earning $200,000 a year, most of it from concert appearances. That year, he formed Acuff-Rose Publishing with songwriter Fred Rose. It became the first major song publisher in Nashville. Now owned by Opryland Music, it remains one of the most successful and historically important companies in country music. Acuff and Wesley Rose (Fred's son) also started Hickory Records in 1957.

Acuff ran for governor of Tennessee in 1944 and 1948, losing each time in the predominantly Democratic state. But his musical career continued to ride high. During World War II, when Japanese troops stormed Okinawa, they were reported to shout, "To hell with Roosevelt! To hell with

Acuff suggested to Opry management in the late 1980s that it might be time for him to retire. The Opry felt differently, and Acuff continued to perform into the 1990s.

song now closely identified with Acuff. But the 1936 version features band member Sam "Dynamite" Hatcher on vocals. Though Acuff performed the song from the time he joined the Opry, he didn't record it as a vocalist until 1947.

In 1939, amid the Opry's move to promote Acuff and itself, NBC Radio decided to air a half-hour segment of the Opry each Saturday night. Acuff and the Smoky Mountain Boys played the opening and closing numbers, which gave them national exposure just as radio was expanding across America. The singer made the best of the opportunity, blending humble comments and warm introductions with devout mountain gospel songs and passionate tales of love and heartbreak. He also received fine assistance from his band, which featured Pete "Bashful Brother Oswald" Kirby on dobro, Jess Easterday on bass, Rachel Veach on banjo, and Lonnie

Babe Ruth! To hell with Roy Acuff!" At about the same time, baseball star Dizzy Dean proclaimed Acuff as "the King of Country Music," a title he maintains to this day.

A dispute with the Opry prompted Acuff to leave in 1946, and he was briefly replaced as host by Red Foley. But Acuff returned the next year, celebrated his 50th anniversary with the program in 1988, and was still the Opry's host in 1992.

Acuff did not achieve great radio airplay or record sales after the mid-1940s, though his songs continued to periodically appear on the charts as late as 1974. This

Acuff's long-lived appeal stems from his blending of a sincere vocal style with a flair for showmanship. On stage, he wields his fiddle bow like a master, waving it over his head, balancing it on his nose, or simply holding it with reverence.

career downturn occurred because Acuff never altered his musical style over the years, clinging instead to the old-style mountain music he originally performed.

However, Acuff's position as the dean of Opry performers has kept him in the limelight. He was elected to the Country Music Hall of Fame in 1962, becoming its first living member.

ROY ACUFF

Real name: Roy Claxton Acuff
Born: September, 15, 1903; Maynardville, Tennessee
First hit: "The Great Speckled Bird" (1937)
Other notable hits: "The Wabash Cannon Ball" (1938), "Ida Red" (1939), "When I Lay My Burden Down" (1940), "Wreck on the Highway" (1942), "Fireball Mail" (1942), "Night Train to Memphis" (1943)
Awards and achievements: Grand Ole Opry member (1938); Country Music Hall of Fame (1962); Kennedy Center honor (1991)

SONS OF THE PIONEERS WITH ROY ROGERS

The Sons of the Pioneers got together in 1933 and have survived endless personnel changes; the name continues today. From the start, the group's hallmark was gentle, pretty harmonies and songs that evoke the romance of the Old West. Here, Roy Rogers (left) is joined at a recording session by his wife, Dale Evans.

The Sons of the Pioneers represent the cream of western music. The group featured the musical genre's most famous singer, its most evocative and accomplished songwriter, and the smoothest three-part harmonies this side of the Pearly Gates.

Group founders included Leonard Slye, who changed his name to Roy Rogers when he signed a motion picture contract with Republic Pictures in 1937; songwriter-singer Bob Nolan, who wrote "Cool Water" and "Tumbling Tumbleweeds," arguably the best (and best-known) of all western songs; and Tim Spencer.

The group formed in late 1933 in California after the three members had skipped through several other vocal groups. Rogers, who was born in Cincinnati, Ohio, in 1912, moved to California with his father to look for work in 1930.

Nolan was born in Canada in 1908 and moved to Tucson, Arizona, at age 14, where he was awestruck by the desert and its stark beauty. Spencer was born in 1905 and was from Missouri.

Originally known as the Pioneer Trio, the group added instrumentalists Hugh and Karl Farr in 1934 shortly after changing the group's name to Sons of the Pioneers. They began performing six days a week on a Los Angeles radio station, and became a popular hit.

Gene Autry, who helped create the cowboy music craze, started as a movie star and then made records. The Sons of the Pioneers came to the movies after scoring musical hits. When Autry left Republic Pictures in a contract dispute in 1937, the studio lured Rogers into leaving the group to sign a movie contract.

His first movie, *Under the Western Stars,* was an immediate hit. Unlike many of his pictures that followed, it had a serious undertone involving farmers who were financially devastated by dust storms. The movie's theme song, "Dust," earned an Academy Award nomination for composer Johnny Marvin.

Within a few years, Rogers ranked as America's number-one box office attraction. He went on to star in 81 movies and 101 television episodes, frequently with his wife, Dale Evans. In time, Roy Rogers became one of the most respected and beloved personalities in America. His old bandmates appeared in several of his movies, as well as with John Wayne and Gene Autry. The films and TV episodes remain popular, so Rogers's star has not dimmed.

Rogers remained on friendly terms with the Pioneers. Nolan and Spencer contributed songs to Rogers's solo recordings and occasionally backed him in the studio. Meanwhile, the members continued on their own, evolving through several personnel changes over the years. A latter-day incarnation of the Sons of the Pioneers was still touring in the 1990s.

The Pioneers made frequent appearances over the years in western movies. Although Roy Rogers was the only member to go on to solo film stardom, Ken Curtis (top, center) eventually found great success as Festus on TV's Gunsmoke.

SONS OF THE PIONEERS WITH ROY ROGERS

Real names: Leonard Slye (Roy Rogers); Robert Clarence Nobles (Bob Nolan); Tim Spencer

Born: (Rogers) November 5, 1912; Cincinnati, Ohio
(Nolan) April 1, 1908; New Brunswick, Canada
(Spencer) July 7, 1905; Webb City, Missouri

Died: (Nolan) June 16, 1980; Los Angeles, California
(Spencer) April 26, 1974; Apple Valley, California

First hit: "Tumbling Tumbleweeds" (1934)

Other notable hits: "Stars and Stripes on Iwo Jima" (1945), "Teardrops in My Heart" (1947), "Baby Doll" (1947), "Cool Water" (1948), "Room Full of Roses" (1949)

Awards and achievements: Western Heritage Award (1971); Country Music Hall of Fame (1980)

Tex Ritter was a fourth-generation Texan who came to epitomize the Hollywood cowboy hero: A rugged individualist with a moral streak and a way with a guitar. Here, he serenades actress Louise Stanley on the set of the 1937 film, Riders of the Rockies.

Tex Ritter left home hoping to become a lawyer. He drew standing ovations singing in a Broadway musical. He gained nationwide stardom acting in cowboy movies. But, first and foremost, he will be remembered as a country and western singing star.

He was born Woodward Maurice Ritter in 1905 in Murvaul, Texas, and raised on land his great-grandfather settled in 1830. As a youngster, he enjoyed sitting in courtrooms listening to lawyers argue cases. After gaining a political science degree at the University of Texas, he was admitted into the law school at Northwestern University near Chicago. However, he couldn't afford to maintain his studies and returned to Texas.

Music had long been Ritter's hobby. He could play guitar and trumpet, he collected folk songs, and he had been president of the Univerisity of Texas glee club. He combined these interests by singing cowboy songs on his own Houston radio show in 1928. The program's success led to extensive concert tours of the South and Midwest.

His ambition led to a move to New York City, where he was cast in a Broadway play, *Green Grow the Lilacs*. The show was transformed into the musical *Oklahoma!*, and Ritter performed four songs in the original production. His memorable role led to a new nickname, Tex.

His Broadway success led to roles in other plays and on several New York radio shows. Then Grand National Pictures hired him to follow in the tradition of the first cowboy movie star, Gene Autry, who worked for a rival studio. Between 1936 and 1945, Ritter starred in more than 60 movies. He had a keen interest in western lore, and he worked to make his pictures and his music more realistic than the competition's. He introduced several of his well-known songs in the movies, including "Rye Whiskey," "Bad Brahma Bull," and "Blood on the Saddle."

Above: *Although a cowboy star, Ritter was also an educated, cosmopolitan man who made his mark in many different facets of show business.* Below: *He began wearing white Stetson hats in Hollywood, and they quickly became a trademark.*

In 1941, Ritter married actress Dorothy Fay, who appeared with him in several movies. The following year, he became the first country artist signed to Capitol Records. In 1952, he was asked to sing the title song for the film *High Noon.* His unique rendition garnered the composers an Academy Award for Best Song. In 1958 Ritter became host of the TV series *Ranch Party.*

Ritter was inducted into the Country Music Hall of Fame in 1964, and the following year he moved to Nashville to join the Grand Ole Opry.

Ritter pursued a lifelong ambition to work in politics by running unsuccessfully for the U.S. Senate seat in Tennessee in 1971. He died of a heart attack on January 2, 1974, while bailing a friend out of jail. His son, John Ritter, went on to star in television and movies.

TEX RITTER

Real name: Woodward Maurice Ritter

Born: January 12, 1905; Murvaul, Texas

Died: January 2, 1974; Nashville, Tennessee

First hit: "Get Along, Little Dogies" (1931)

Other notable hits: "Jingle Jangle Jingle" (1942), "Boll Weevil Song" (1946), "Blood on the Saddle" (1946), "Rye Whiskey" (1948), "High Noon (Do Not Forsake Me)" (1952), "I Dreamed of a Hillbilly Heaven" (1961)

Awards and achievements: Recorded Academy Award winner, Best Song (1953); Country Music Hall of Fame (1964); Grand Ole Opry member (1965)

BOB WILLS

Above: *Bob Wills and His Texas Playboys, early in the band's career. Wills formed the group in 1933, incorporating horns, reeds, and drummer Smokey Dacus—all unusual elements for country bands of the time.* Opposite: *Handsome and musically innovative, Wills struggled for years to keep his personal life on an even keel.*

Bob Wills remains country music's greatest bandleader, as well as one of its most innovative, progressive musical visionaries. He didn't exactly create the musical style called western swing, though he was among a community of musicians who forged this new, lively blend in the early 1930s. But one fact is indisputable: Wills and his band, the Texas Playboys, are responsible for making western swing a popular American musical style.

Wills was born in 1905 in Kosse, Texas, and raised on the western side of the state in a town called Turkey. His father was an accomplished breakdown fiddler, and the young Wills often joined his father at barn dances and house parties.

In his teen years, Wills was a wild, restless sort who didn't pursue music or any other profession for long. He traveled Texas as a hobo in the 1920s, working odd jobs. He spent time as a farmer and a barber before leaving Turkey for good after an arrest for public rowdiness. He decided to trade on his musical upbringing by joining a medicine show, where he gained a wider exposure to blues, swing, Dixieland, and other musical styles.

He arrived in Fort Worth in 1929 and hooked up with guitarist Herman Arnspiger. Along with another friend, singer Milton Brown, Wills and Arnspiger found work on a radio show. Because they plugged Light Crust Flour for boss W. Lee O'Daniel—who later was elected governor of Texas—Wills and his friends became known as the Light Crust Doughboys.

Milton Brown left the group in 1932 to form Milton Brown and His Musical Brownies, credited by some as the first western swing band. Wills departed the following

ROOTS: THE 1920s AND 1930s

Wills (front left, black hat) appeared in western movies, including Take Me Back to Oklahoma, *a 1940 vehicle for Tex Ritter (center).*

year with singer Tommy Duncan to form a new band. Unfortunately, each time they found employment at a radio station, O'Daniel would see to it that they were fired. So Wills, Duncan, and the others moved to Tulsa, Oklahoma, to take a job with 50,000-watt KVOO.

Wills dubbed his band the Texas Playboys, and from 1934 to 1940 the group performed daily on KVOO, then entertained dance crowds nightly at the expansive Cain's Academy ballroom in downtown Tulsa. In 1935, Wills hired Smokey Dacus, making him

the first drummer in a major country music outfit. He then added a horn section. From that point on, Wills increasingly emphasized dance rhythms and swinging, hot musicianship.

Wills's own fiddle playing drew on the traditional breakdown style he learned in his youth. When he blended that sound with the swing and Dixieland jazz sweeping the United States, he created a bopping style unique to the Southwest. Wills liked the blues of Bessie Smith, the smooth pop of Bing Crosby, the swing of Tommy Dorsey and Benny Goodman, and

the rhythmic drive of Count Basie and Earl "Fatha" Hines. He incorporated these styles with the polkas and waltzes of the German immigrants in Texas and with the pulse of Tex-Mex accordion music. It was a swinging hodge podge that Wills was clever enough to temper with the supple baritone of Duncan, who remained a Playboy until 1948.

Wills led his band with an entertaining charisma and bawdy dynamism. He strutted the stage during concerts, dressed as a stylish uptown Texan and chomping on a cigar as he pointed to musicians for their solos. Despite his cavalier presence, he attracted top musicians and demanded originality and innovation. He also gave them room to play and allowed them to take part in arranging the music.

The musicians featured in the Texas Playboys over the years include fiddlers Jesse Ashlock, Louis Tierney, Joe Holley, and Johnny Gimble, who provided jazzy inflections while helping Wills achieve his famed twin-fiddle sound. Al Stricklin was a longtime Playboy pianist, and Eldon Shamblin and Junior Barnard were among those who followed Herman Arnspiger on guitar. Leon McAuliffe helped popularize the steel guitar with his work as a Playboy, and Tiny Moore brought new innovations to the electric mandolin. Leon Rausch is among the singers who followed Duncan.

The Playboys' first recording sessions took place in 1935 with an 11-piece band and Wills was a major music star by 1940, when he and the Playboys were invited to appear in the first of several western movies.

Even as Wills's professional life was thriving, his personal life was often a shambles. He was a restless man even at the height of his success, and he went on alcoholic binges throughout his life. He divorced his first wife in 1936, then weathered three unsuccessful marriages in the ensuing five years.

He married Betty Anderson in 1942, and the relationship lasted 33 years. That same year, he joined the U.S. Army. Thirty-eight years old and accustomed to calling his own shots, he was discharged after seven months. Wills then moved to California, taking a few musicians

Wills grew up in West Texas but spent most of his adult life in more sophisticated surroundings. Still, when called upon, he could play up his Southwestern roots.

with him and hiring the rest in Los Angeles. He enjoyed great success at that point, acquiring wealth and the respect of musicians outside of country music.

Wills and the Texas Playboys recorded their most famous work between the late 1930s and early 1950s, though he continued to record periodically into the 1960s. In 1968, he was elected to the Country Music Hall of Fame. His last studio appearance came during a 1973 reunion of the Texas Playboys. During the sessions, Wills suffered a stroke and slipped into a coma. He died in 1975.

BOB WILLS

Real name: James Robert Wills

Born: March 6, 1905; Kosse, Texas

Died: May 13, 1975; Fort Worth, Texas

First hit: "Spanish Two Step" (1936)

Other notable hits: "Right or Wrong" (1937), "New San Antonio Rose" (1940), "Stay a Little Longer" (1946), "Faded Love" (1950)

Awards and achievements: Country Music Hall of Fame (1968); Academy of Country Music Pioneer Award (1969)

In the late 1930s, several important factors pointed country music toward its future as a prominent entertainment form. Gene Autry sauntered onto the American landscape as a film star by portraying a solid, heroic figure of the Old West who dressed in fancy cowboy duds and crooned romantic, wistful songs about open spaces and long-lasting love. At the same time, the ascendant jukebox popularized dance halls and juke joints as social gathering places where the music needed to be loud enough to be heard over a crowd and rhythmic enough to keep dancers moving. And the NBC radio network began a national broadcast of a portion of the Grand Ole Opry each Saturday night, taking the sound of Nashville and the rural South into millions of homes.

Roy Rogers, seen here with wife Dale Evans, had early success as a vocalist with the Sons of the Pioneers and went on to enormous screen and TV stardom.

By the 1940s, Gene Autry had been joined by several other western singing stars. Foremost among them was Roy Rogers ("the King of the Cowboys") and his early musical partners, the Sons of the Pioneers. The latter group is widely considered as the epitome of western music as an art form, and Rogers is the soloist who went on to the widest national fame. There were others: Tex Ritter, Johnny Bond, Jimmy Wakely, Elton Britt, Stuart Hamblen, and Rex Allen also sang of tumblin' tumbleweeds.

The jukebox, meanwhile, nurtured a more raucous, harder-edged style of country music, and the nightlife it encouraged brought with it new topics for songwriters. Wurlitzer introduced the jukebox in 1928, and the machine's popularity grew as the Depression and Prohibition waned. By 1940, more than 300,000 portable jukeboxes were in operation. With it, the beat of Southern music picked up its tempo, and the piano, the string bass, the electric guitar, and the steel guitar joined the fiddle as primary country music instruments.

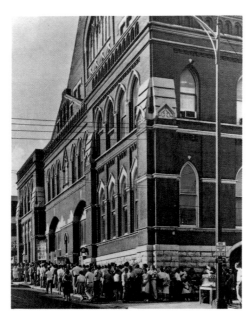

The Grand Ole Opry moved into Nashville's Ryman Auditorium in 1943 and remained there until 1974. The site is still revered as a shrine of country music.

In addition, the onslaught of World War II and the great influx of American men into the armed services allowed an unprecedented mingling of regional cultures. New musical influences were shared and fresh styles were discovered.

The louder music and new lifestyles broadened the lyrical topics, too. Songwriters focused less on God, family, and home and began to explore the insecurities of love, the varying levels of guilt, and the joys and dangers of drinking, rambling, and other means of escape.

Two musical styles emerged in country music during the forties: gritty, song-based honky-tonk and freewheeling, instrumentally daring western swing. Both forms produced pioneers and heroes. In honky-tonk, they included Ernest Tubb, Hank Williams, Floyd Tillman, Moon Mullican, and Ted Daffan. In western swing, the list is headed by Bob Wills and His Texas Playboys, Milton Brown and His Musical Brownies, and Spade Cooley.

Far left: *Patsy Cline's versatile, melodious voice propelled her to country stardom in the late 1950s.* Above: *Heartfelt songs and a remarkable vocal style characterize Hank Williams. His musical legacy is unmatched.*

Meanwhile, as country music's popularity grew, so did the means of marketing, distribution, and personal appearances. Of the many radio centers that attracted developing musical talent, Nashville was particularly vigorous, and began its rise as the capital of country music. The Opry gained a major foothold thanks to NBC and a heavily promoted touring schedule that featured financial assistance from companies such as tobacco giant R.J. Reynolds. The Opry also attained a reputation as home of country music's biggest stars, starting with Roy Acuff and growing to include Ernest Tubb, Eddy Arnold, Hank Williams, Red Foley, Webb Pierce, Kitty Wells, Hank Snow, Jim Reeves, Marty Robbins, and others.

Expanding from the WSM base, Roy Acuff and veteran New York songwriter Fred Rose started Nashville's first major music publishing company, Acuff-Rose. Then Decca Records prudently decided to produce records in the city where many country music stars were centered. After Decca hired Owen Bradley to produce sides by Ernest Tubb and Red Foley, other companies followed suit.

By the 1950s, the term "country music" encompassed a wide variety of styles. There was the bluegrass of Bill Monroe, Flatt & Scruggs, and the Stanley Brothers; the traditional mountain sound of Acuff, Wells, the Louvin Brothers, Molly O'Day, and Wilma Lee and Stoney Cooper; the honky-tonk of Williams, Lefty Frizzell, Pierce, Ray Price, George Jones, and Faron Young; and the smoother, pop leanings of Arnold, Reeves, Robbins, Slim Whitman, Sonny James, and Patsy Cline.

The music of Nashville struggled to maintain an audience as the rock 'n' roll era took hold, and the resulting insecurity created an era of experimentation. By and large, the modern sounds of honky-tonk and country-pop proved more commercially durable than the traditional approach. But the tensions that remained have continued to mark this roots-based, encompassing musical genre in the ensuing decades.

In country music, there seems to be only one truism: New songs and new artists will forever be judged against the passionate, personal, and pioneering music developed in the South during the 1940s and 1950s.

Below: *Lefty Frizzell's modulated vocal style seems to sum up the sound of country, and has influenced many singers who came later.*

Bill Monroe (second from left) performs with an early incarnation of the Bluegrass Boys shortly after joining the Grand Ole Opry in 1939. His band featured Art Wooten on fiddle, Cleo Davis on guitar, and Amos Garen on bass. (Garen had been preceded by John Miller on the jug.) Monroe's mandolin and vocals dominated the group, and set the standard for all bluegrass music that followed.

A few country music figures can claim to have helped popularize or revive a particular style of music. Only Bill Monroe can take credit for *creating* a distinct musical form. When Monroe is called "The Father of Bluegrass Music," it's not an overstatement. He forged an individual musical style out of an amalgam of old-time mountain music, Holiness Church gospel, blues, and jazz that attracted a school of imitators and

inspired a new genre of music. It came to be known as bluegrass because Monroe called his band the Bluegrass Boys, after a famous aspect of his native state, Kentucky.

Monroe was born in 1911 on a farm near Rosine in Western Kentucky. His poor eyesight led to a reclusive devotion to music, and he developed into an expert on the mandolin, fiddle, and guitar. His mother, an old-time fiddler, died

when Monroe was ten. His father died six years later, and the young Monroe moved in with his uncle Pendleton Vandiver, an accomplished musician.

In the late 1920s, Bill joined with older brothers Charlie and Birch to play at square dances during their spare time. When full-time radio work was offered in 1934, Birch left the group, leaving Bill and Charlie as the Monroe Brothers duet. The pair found

Monroe was 67 when this photograph was taken in October of 1978. Now in his 80s, he continues to perform regularly across the United States.

success in radio and as recording artists with Victor Records between 1936 and 1938. The brothers split in 1938, with Charlie forming the Kentucky Pardners and Bill organizing his first Bluegrass Boys band.

At that point, Bill Monroe set out to create a more aggressive, hard-driving style of music. He pushed the mandolin, banjo and fiddle into lead instruments, demanding that his musicians excel at nimble ensemble playing and flashy, improvisational solos.

In 1939, he joined the Grand Ole Opry; his debut performance featured his first famous song, "New Mule Skinner Blues." The following year, he signed with Victor Records; his second session included the second known recording of the bluegrass standard "Orange Blossom Special."

Two of the Bluegrass Boys, banjoist Earl Scruggs and singer-guitarist Lester Flatt, split with Monroe in 1950 to go solo.

Monroe was so bitter about the duo's departure that he left his record company because the label signed Flatt and Scruggs to a contract.

Though never a popular radio artist, Monroe has maintained a small, fervent following, and those he has influenced include George Jones, Elvis Presley, and Bob Dylan. He also received a boost in recognition during the folk music boom in the late 1950s and early 1960s. He remained active into his eighties, performing regularly on the Opry and at bluegrass festivals. He was elected to the Country Music Hall of Fame in 1970.

BILL MONROE

Real name: William Smith Monroe

Born: September 13, 1911; Rosine, Kentucky

First hit: "New Mule Skinner Blues" (1939)

Other notable hits: "Orange Blossom Special" (1940), "Blue Moon of Kentucky" (1946), "Kentucky Waltz" (1946), "Uncle Pen" (1950), "Walk Softly on This Heart of Mine" (1969)

Awards and achievements: Country Music Hall of Fame (1970); Grammy Award, Best Bluegrass Recording (1988)

Bill Monroe on his Tennessee farm, 1971. He has weathered several downturns in popularity over the decades, but musically he maintained high quality while never straying too far from the bluegrass sound he created.

EDDY ARNOLD

Eddy Arnold stands as country music's most successful crooner, and his longevity ranks him as one of America's most enduring hitmakers. Arnold was neither hillbilly nor honky-tonk. Though he was rural raised, the "Tennessee Plowboy" sang without a Southern drawl and openly embraced pop influences. He was country music's first crossover king, a smooth balladeer who appealed not only to country fans but also to those who couldn't relate to Hank Williams's rustic inflections or who cringed at Roy Acuff's pinched tenor.

Arnold was born in 1918 near Henderson, Tennessee, where his father was a sharecropper and an old-time fiddler. He performed music regularly in high school, though he had to drop out to work on the farm before graduating.

Music grew from sideline to profession when he found a job performing at a radio station in nearby Jackson. He also worked for stations in Memphis and St. Louis before joining Pee Wee King and the Golden West Cowboys in the early 1940s. By 1944, Arnold had a solo contract with RCA Records and had become one of the Opry's leading attractions. The following year he recorded the first version of his theme song, "Cattle Call."

In 1945, Arnold acquired a new manager, Col. Tom Parker, who later would gain fame managing Elvis Presley. Two years later, Arnold attained his first number one hit, and for the next 20 years he was country music's most successful record maker. Through the mid-1950s, he regularly had two or three songs in the Top 10 at the same time.

Billboard magazine ranked him as the most successful country recording artist in the 1940s. He was ranked second for the 1950s, then sixth in the 1960s. His 1947 hit, "I'll Hold You in My Heart," ties the record for the most consecutive weeks at Number One with 21. "Bouquet of Roses" spent 54 weeks in the country music Top 40, another long-standing record yet to be broken.

Active on the personal-appearance circuit and a frequent presence on television variety shows, Arnold hosted four different variety programs in the 1950s, logging time on all three networks as well as starring in his own syndicated series. Since then, he has hosted more than 20 TV specials.

The singer aged well, scoring major hits into the 1970s. As late as 1967, he was rated as top country artist of the year according to his showing on the *Billboard* charts. Fifty years after joining the Pee Wee King band, Arnold was still performing sporadically.

Eddy Arnold, 1950. Of the major country performers who emerged in the early 1940s, he is the only one who continues to tour and perform; he favors extended runs in supper theaters and concert halls.

EDDY ARNOLD

Real name: Richard Edward Arnold

Born: May 15, 1918; Henderson, Tennessee

First hit: "Each Minute Seems Like a Million Years" (1945)

Notable hits: "I'll Hold You in My Heart (Till I Can Hold You in My Arms)" (1947), "Bouquet of Roses" (1948), "Anytime" (1948), "I Wanna Play House with You" (1951), "I Really Don't Want to Know" (1954), "Make the World Go Away" (1965)

Awards and achievements: Top country singles artist of all time; top country artist of 1940s; longest-remaining song in country Top 40 ("Bouquet of Roses"); Grand Ole Opry member (1942-1948); Country Music Hall of Fame (1966)

An innovative and influential guitarist, Merle Travis also made his mark as a songwriter. The country classics he wrote include "Sixteen Tons," "Nine Pound Hammer," and "Divorce Me C.O.D."

Merle Travis is perhaps best remembered as an innovative, groundbreaking guitarist. But the versatile Kentucky native also was an accomplished songwriter and singer who mastered honky-tonk, western swing, and folk music with style.

Travis was born in 1917 in the small town of Rosewood in the coal-mining area of Muhlenberg County, Kentucky. He began playing guitar as a youngster, and by adulthood he had perfected a regional style of picking that used the thumb to play rhythm on the bass strings and the index finger to play the melody on the treble strings. It has become a frequently emulated style that is known as "Travis Picking."

After recording with Grandpa Jones and the Delmore Brothers in Cincinnati, Travis moved to the West Coast, where in 1946 Capitol Records offered him a recording contract after he played on a Tex Ritter session. Travis's earliest solo recordings were folk-based tunes done at the request of Capitol, and they included the original versions of such Travis compositions as "Sixteen Tons," "Dark as a Dungeon," and "I Am a Pilgrim." He also wrote "Smoke! Smoke! Smoke! (That Cigarette)," which gave Tex Williams a hit and Capitol its first million-seller.

As a performer, Travis moved on to record his most famous solo country hits, including "Divorce Me C.O.D.," "So Round, So Firm, So Fully Packed," "No Vacancy," "Three Times Seven," and "Fat Gal." These witty novelty tunes featured the unusual touches of trumpet and accordion, as well as fiddles and guitars.

Travis—one of the most innovative guitarists of his era—was elected to the Country Music Hall of Fame in 1977. He died in 1983 in Oklahoma.

MERLE TRAVIS

Real name: Merle Robert Travis

Born: November 29, 1917; Rosewood, Kentucky

Died: October 20, 1983; Tahlequah, Oklahoma

First hit: "Cincinnati Lou" (1946)

Other notable hits: "Divorce Me C.O.D." (1946), "So Round, So Firm, So Fully Packed" (1947), "Steel Guitar Rag" (1947), "Three Times Seven" (1947), "Fat Gal" (1947), "Merle's Boogie Woogie" (1948)

Awards and achievements: Nashville Songwriters Hall of Fame (1970); Country Music Hall of Fame (1977); Influential Guitar Stylist

ERNEST TUBB

A star for more than 40 years, Ernest Tubb was a distinctive song stylist who overcame the limits of his baritone by singing with heart and warmth.

Ernest Tubb didn't always hit the right notes, but he struck a deep chord in listeners, proving that a singer with a limited vocal range could achieve unlimited success in country music. His remarkable baritone was warm, earthy, and thoroughly natural, and he used it to intimately communicate his lyrics.

Tubb was born in 1914 on a farm near Crisp, Texas, and he grew up with a succession of relatives after his parents separated. He decided to become a singer at age 14, after hearing Jimmie Rodgers. By 1933, Tubb had moved to San Antonio and, while working for the WPA, talked his way into a singing job on radio station KONO. The next year he met Carrie Rodgers, his idol's widow. Impressed by his dedication, she landed Tubb a contract with Victor Records and made him a present of her husband's valuable guitar.

Following a tonsillectomy that severely affected his voice, Tubb joined Decca Records in 1940 and recorded his breakthrough hit, "Walking the Floor Over You," a year later. He joined the Grand Ole Opry in January 1943 and appeared in two western movies with star Charles Starrett. Tubb also appeared in two low-budget musicals, *Jamboree* (1943) and *Hollywood Barn Dance* (1947).

Tubb was a trailblazer, as well as a congenial and generous mentor to scores of musicians and country artists. He was an architect of what became known as the honky-tonk sound, partly because he was among the first country stars to use an electric guitar as a musical focal point. He had made the move in 1941 when a nightclub owner complained that jukebox records couldn't be heard once a crowd grew animated. He added a drum kit in 1949, another rarity for a Grand Ole Opry performer at the time.

Tubb was the first major country music artist to record regularly in Nashville, thereby helping establish the city as a leading recording center. His insistence on recording in Nashville also led Decca Records to open a branch office in that city. When other companies followed, the foundation was set for what is now known as Music City U.S.A.

Tubb opened his landmark Ernest Tubb Record Store in downtown Nashville in the late 1940s (it now is a four-store chain and an active mail-order business). At the same time, he started the *Midnight Jamboree* radio show, still broadcast each Saturday following the Grand Ole Opry.

Tubb was inducted into the Country Music Hall of Fame in 1965. He maintained a steady touring schedule into his seventies, despite contracting emphysema. He died in 1984.

ERNEST TUBB

Born: February 9, 1914; Crisp, Texas

Died: September 6, 1984; Nashville, Tennessee

First hit: "Walking the Floor Over You" (1941)

Other notable hits: "It's Been So Long, Darling" (1945), "Tomorrow Never Comes" (1945), "Drivin' Nails in My Coffin" (1946), "Let's Say Goodbye Like We Said Hello" (1948), "Thanks a Lot" (1963), "Waltz Across Texas" (1965)

Awards and achievements: Grand Ole Opry member (1943); Country Music Hall of Fame (1965); Academy of Country Music Pioneer Award (1980)

Above: *Tubb joined Decca Records in 1940 and issued his breakthrough smash, "Walking the Floor Over You," a year later.*
Opposite: *Tubb spent prodigious amounts of time on the road, so at-home images such as this are rare.*

CLASSICS: THE 1940s AND 1950s

39

Left: *The fervent and intensely creative Hank Williams, in his best-known publicity photograph.* Opposite: *Williams lets loose in Columbus, Ohio, in October of 1951. His appearance was part of a country music tour sponsored by Hadacol, a health tonic later banned by the government.*

Hank Williams will forever represent the essence of country music. He grew up poor in rural Alabama, yet he rose to become the biggest star of his generation. He couldn't write a literate letter, yet he composed classic songs filled with power and simple truth. He climbed far beyond his dreams, yet he lived a tortured existence racked with pain, sorrow, and guilt. His music was loved by millions, yet at age 29 he died of a drug and alcohol overdose in the back seat of a Cadillac driven by a stranger.

He was born Hiriam Williams on September 17, 1923, on a tenant farm outside of Mount Olive, Alabama. His father, Elonzo Williams, was a shell-shocked veteran of World War I. His mother, Lillian Skipper Williams, was an imposing, domineering woman who separated from her husband in 1929 and later ran a dreary, hard-knocks boarding house in Montgomery, Alabama. She raised her son in the fundamentalist Baptist tradition. The boy hated the name Hiriam, a misspelling of the biblical King Hiram, and preferred Hank.

He learned guitar before he was ten years old, but he cited his early teen experiences with a black street singer named Tee-Tot (Rufe Payne) as the seasoning that taught him to put feeling into his music. Williams dogged Tee-Tot on the streets of Greenville, Alabama, giving him money he made shining shoes to learn blues chords and old folk songs. "Colored music is real natural," he later told interviewer Melvin Shestack.

Williams won a talent contest at age 14 with his composition, "WPA Blues." He soon was performing at barn dances, school parties, and in honky-tonks, traveling as far as Florida for bookings. Settling in Texas at 17, he put together a band, the Drifting Cowboys. Although his songs had little connection to the prairie sound of cowboy music, he loved cowboy lore, and always cited the Texas honky-tonk sound of Ernest Tubb as an overriding influence. The keening rhythms of Lone Star swing, combined with the stark emotionalism of Southeastern country music, were the foundations of the Hank Williams sound.

Back in Alabama, he auditioned for Montgomery's WSFA radio and soon became a featured singer

Alabama teenager Hank Williams, at a time when he performed on the streets of Montgomery and Greenville.

His fourth recording for Sterling was his composition "Honky Tonkin'." Its success led to interest from nationally positioned MGM Records, and in April 1947 Williams recorded "Move It On Over" for that label. Within a year, the record sold 108,000 copies.

Williams was on his way. In August 1948 he joined the *Louisiana Hayride* radio show in Shreveport. Though the program had only started the previous April, it was broadcast on a clear-channel station that reached a large weekend audience throughout the South and Midwest.

In February 1949, Williams released "Lovesick Blues," a song from a 1922 musical he first heard on a Rex Griffin record. It was Hank's first number-one record, and one of country radio's biggest hits of all time, spending 16 weeks at the top spot and an incredible 42 weeks on the country charts. It sold more than three million copies.

In May 1949, while "Lovesick Blues" was entrenched at number one, Randall Hank Williams was born. Two weeks after his son's birth, Williams accepted an invitation to join the Grand Ole Opry. The family moved to Nashville and built a $50,000 home on Franklin Road, not far from the offices of Acuff-Rose.

For the next three years, Hank Williams was country music's dominant figure. His hits during that period included "Mind Your Own Business," "My Bucket's Got a Hole in It," "I Don't Like This Kind of Livin'," "Long Gone Lonesome Blues," "Why Don't You Love Me," "Moanin' the Blues," "Cold, Cold Heart," "I Can't Help It (If I'm Still in Love with You)," "Hey, Good Lookin',"

on the station. The job led to broader concert bookings, and, while performing in Banks, Alabama, he met his future wife, Audrey.

Meanwhile, Williams's reputation grew. He performed as the local opening act for Grand Ole Opry package tours in Alabama, where he met Roy Acuff and sold a song to Opry star Pee Wee King. He also was building another reputation: as a problem drinker

who wasn't always reliable.

He married Audrey in 1944 at a filling station in Andalusia, Alabama. His wife stoked his ambition, encouraging him to go to Nashville. Fred Rose of Acuff-Rose had shown interest in his songs, and after the first Nashville trip in 1946, Rose signed Williams to a song publishing contract. Early the next year, Williams recorded for Sterling Records, backed by the Willis Brothers.

Williams (left) with several Grand Ole Opry stars and executives. Milton Estes stands in Hank's shadow; continuing to the right from Estes the group includes Red Foley, Minnie Pearl, Variety's *George Rosen, Wally Fowler (kneeling), Harry Stone, Eddy Arnold, Roy Acuff, Rod Brasfield, and Lew Childre.*

Williams's music, though created in a short period of time, spans a remarkable breadth of styles. He wrote religious songs, mother songs, party songs, and rambling songs. Some of his tunes can be seen as precursors of rockabilly, and the smooth versions of his tunes by pop crooners like Tony Bennett and Joni James set the tone for the cosmopolitan country music that followed. His blend of blues rhythms and poor-white anxiety remain a bedrock of traditional country music, as does his combination of fiddles and slap bass with electric and pedal steel guitars.

In 1961, Williams joined Jimmie Rodgers and mentor Fred Rose as the first three inductees into the Country Music Hall of Fame. More importantly, his lyrical images of the lonesome sound of a distant train whistle or of a moon slipping behind a cloud to cry will eternally serve as reflections of the despair hidden in the human heart.

"Honky Tonk Blues," "Half as Much," "Jambalaya," and "Settin' the Woods on Fire."

However, as his fame increased, his personal life deteriorated. In 1952, he left the house he shared with Audrey and moved in with young Ray Price, then a struggling newcomer. The pair became notorious for their wild parties. Williams grew more erratic and unreliable, and the Opry dropped him from its ranks in August 1952.

On October 19, 1952, Williams married Billie Jean Jones, who was on a date with Faron Young when Williams met her. Their wedding took place three times, once with a justice of the peace and twice before a sold-out auditorium in New Orleans.

Williams spent Christmas of 1952 visiting his mother in Montgomery and his father in southern Alabama. His last public performance took place on December 28 at the Elite Cafe in Montgomery in a benefit for the local American Federation of Musicians union. He died on December 31, 1952, on his way to a New Year's Day show in Canton, Ohio. Heavily medicated, he had been drinking for days. A driver who had been hired the day before to pilot Williams's Cadillac found him slumped in the car's back seat. More than 10,000 people attended his funeral at a Montgomery auditorium.

The week before Williams died, his song "I'll Never Get Out of This World Alive" reached number one on the charts. After his death, his hits continued: "Kawliga," "Your Cheatin' Heart," "Take These Chains from My Heart," "I Won't Be Home No More."

HANK WILLIAMS

Real name: Hiriam Williams

Born: September 17, 1923; Mount Olive, Alabama

Died: January 1, 1953; Oak Hill, West Virginia

First hit: "Lovesick Blues" (1949)

Other notable hits: "Cold, Cold Heart" (1951), "I Can't Help It (If I'm Still in Love with You)" (1951), "Hey, Good Lookin'" (1951), "Honky Tonk Blues" (1952), "Jambalaya (On the Bayou)" (1952), "Your Cheatin' Heart" (1953)

Awards and achievements: Grand Ole Opry member (1949); Country Music Hall of Fame (1961)

LEFTY FRIZZELL

Lefty Frizzell enjoyed enormous success in the early 1950s, shortly after rising to national prominence. Because he often struggled with the wild side of life he sometimes described in his songs, the hits became less frequent later in his career. Here, he visits Cleveland radio station WERE.

L efty Frizzell soared to fame at an early age, and though his career slipped as fast as it had climbed, his influence increases with each passing decade. At the start of the 1990s, 40 years after Frizzell's start, many of country music's biggest young stars owe

a direct debt to Frizzell's expressive vocal technique.

He was born William Orville Frizzell in 1928 in Corsicana, Texas. His father, an oil rigger, chased work across Texas and moved the family regularly. His father also loved country music, and young William learned to play guitar to tunes made famous by Jimmie Rodgers and Ernest Tubb.

The young Frizzell obtained his first job as a pre-teen on a children's radio program in El Dorado, Texas. Within a few years he was performing at county fairs, and before he was of legal drinking age he was playing nightclubs and dance halls. He received his nickname because of a mean left hook he used against a bully during a schoolyard fight.

As his voice changed, Lefty found he could no longer yodel, so he cultivated a way of dragging out notes that created a style that has become a bedrock of traditional country male vocalists. Frizzell has been cited by George Jones and Merle Haggard as their primary vocal influence, which led to later emulations by John Anderson, Randy Travis, Clint Black, Alan Jackson, and others.

In the spring of 1950 Frizzell recorded songs that impressed Don Law, head of Columbia Records in Nashville. Frizzell's first single for Columbia was "If You've Got the Money, I've Got the Time," with "I Love You a Thousand Ways" on the B-side. Both became number-one country records and launched Frizzell to instant stardom.

In October 1951, he achieved an unprecedented and still unequaled landmark by placing four songs at once in the country Top 10: "I Want to Be with You Always," "Always Late," "Mom and Dad's Waltz," and "Travellin' Blues."

However, Frizzell dropped from the charts during a period marked by personal problems; his next Top 10 song wouldn't come until 1959, when he recorded another classic, "Long Black Veil." His next major hit came in 1964 and also was his last, "Saginaw, Michigan."

Frizzell continued to tour throughout the 1960s. In 1972, after a long dry spell, he was let go by Columbia Records. He was picked up by ABC Records that same year and began to record some of his most critically acclaimed works. His second ABC album had recently been released when he died in 1975 of complications from a stroke. Frizzell was elected to the Country Music Hall of Fame in 1982.

LEFTY FRIZZELL

Real name: William Orville Frizzell

Born: March 31, 1928; Corsicana, Texas

Died: July 19, 1975; Nashville, Tennessee

First hit: "If You've Got the Money, I've Got the Time" (1950)

Other notable hits: "I Love You a Thousand Ways" (1951), "I Want to Be with You Always" (1951), "Always Late" (1951), "Mom and Dad's Waltz" (1951), "Long Black Veil" (1959), "Saginaw, Michigan" (1964)

Awards and achievements: Four songs simultaneously in *Billboard* Country Top 10 (1951); Country Music Hall of Fame (1982)

Frizzell gazes at his younger self at his home in Beaumont, Texas. A portable reel-to-reel tape recorder rests at his feet. Frizzell's drawling vocal style stretched the syllables of words in a way that gave the lyrics added emotional impact. His innovations can be heard in songs by George Jones, Merle Haggard, Willie Nelson, and Randy Travis.

Sense of style: Webb Pierce shows off his custom-made Pontiac convertible, which featured hundreds of silver dollars mounted in the interior. Other highlights include six-shooters as door handles, a small saddle for an armrest, and hand-tooled cowhide throughout.

Webb Pierce helped establish several country music customs. His hits in the early 1950s instituted the moaning pedal steel sound as a primary component of country music. His lyrical topics of choice often centered on drinking, cheating, jails, and the honky-tonk lifestyle. He wore loud, colorful western suits studded with rhinestones. In his Pontiac, he mounted hundreds of silver dollars into the interior, secured a steer's horns on the hood, fashioned the car seats as saddles, and used six-shooters for door handles. And he was the first Nashville star to install a guitar-shaped swimming pool in his backyard.

Pierce was born near West Monroe, Louisiana, on August 8, 1926. He performed on local radio in nearby Monroe while still in his teens, and moved to Shreveport in the late 1940s. He worked there as a shoe salesman for Sears Roebuck until gaining an invitation to join the *Louisiana Hayride* program on KWKH radio. With his keening high tenor, Pierce soon became one of the Hayride's biggest stars. He also developed several future hitmakers in his band, including Faron Young, Goldie Hill, Jimmy Day, and Floyd Cramer.

In 1951, Pierce switched from the small, independent Pacemaker and Four Star labels to country giant Decca. His first song for Decca, "Wondering," became a number-one hit, as did his next two releases, "That Heart Belongs to Me" and "Back Street Affair." Pierce joined the Grand Ole Opry in 1952 and issued one of his best-known songs, "There Stands the Glass," a year later.

He went on to score more number-one records in the 1950s than any other country performer. In all, Pierce had 13 chart-topping hits. The second performer on the list, Eddy Arnold, had ten. In addition to the four songs listed above, Pierce's number-one hits include, "It's Been So Long," "Slowly," "In the Jailhouse Now," "I Don't Care," "Love, Love, Love," and "Why Baby Why" (duet with Red Sovine). Pierce also recorded hit duets with Kitty Wells.

At the height of his success, Pierce appeared in several Hollywood movies, including *Buffalo Guns*, *Music City U.S.A.*, and *Road to Nashville*. He also was considered a shrewd businessman, co-founding and co-owning one of Nashville's most historic music publishing companies, Cedarwood.

Pierce remained with Decca and its successor, MCA, until 1972, when he switched to Plantation Records. His recording career faded and he lived off investments and business ventures. He underwent heart surgery in 1990 and passed away on February 24, 1991.

WEBB PIERCE

Born: August 8, 1926; West Monroe, Louisiana

Died: February 24, 1991; Nashville, Tennessee

First hit: "Wondering" (1952)

Other notable hits: "Back Street Affair" (1952), "There Stands the Glass" (1953), "Slowly" (1954), "In the Jailhouse Now" (1955), "I Don't Care" (1955), "I Ain't Never" (1959)

Awards and achievements: Top Country Singles Artist of 1950s

Opposite: *By 1956, when this picture was taken, Pierce was among the few country stars creating hard-edged country music that kept a grip on fans at a time when rock 'n' roll was becoming dominant.*

CLASSICS: THE 1940s AND 1950s

Ray Price etched his mark into country history with two distinctively different but equally successful styles. He bopped through the late 1950s with a swinging, hard-edged honky-tonk sound centered on a shuffle rhythm that came to be known as the Ray Price Beat. Then, in the late 1960s, he lowered his voice, traded the fiddles and steel guitars for a violin section and muted guitars, and became one of country music's most successful crooners.

Price was born in 1926 in Perryville, Texas, and grew up in Dallas. In 1949, he quit his studies in veterinary medicine to pursue music full time. In 1951, after two years on the *Big D Jamboree* radio show, Price signed with Columbia Records and moved to Nashville. He joined the Grand Ole Opry in 1952 with help from his friend and roommate, Hank Williams.

Price scored his biggest early hit in 1956 with "Crazy Arms," which introduced his shuffle beat. But by 1967 he devoted himself to a lusher style, starting with a recording of "Danny Boy" that featured a 47-piece orchestra. He continued to have success with his new sound into the 1970s.

Over the years, Price also developed a reputation for finding fresh songs by up-and-coming songwriters. Among the writers he drew from early in their careers were Roger Miller, Willie Nelson, Kris Kristofferson, Mel Tillis, Bill Anderson, Harlan Howard, and Hank Cochran.

Price was still achieving Top 10 hits in the early 1980s, three decades after his start, and he continued to perform regularly in the 1990s.

Above: *Ray Price joined the Grand Ole Opry in 1952 after experience on the Dallas-based* Big D Jamboree *radio show.* Below: *By the 1960s, Price had traded his honky-tonk sound for a smooth country-pop approach.*

RAY PRICE

Real name: Ray Noble Price

Born: January 12, 1926; Perryville, Texas

First hit: "Talk to Your Heart" (1952)

Other notable hits: "Release Me" (1954), "Crazy Arms" (1956), "City Lights" (1958), "Invitation to the Blues" (1958), "Heartaches by the Number" (1959), "For the Good Times" (1970)

Awards and achievements: Grand Ole Opry member (1952); 46 Top 10 hits (1952-1982)

JIM REEVES

Jim Reeves rose from deeply rural roots in the thickets of East Texas to become one of the smoothest, most universally popular country singers of the late 1950s and early 1960s.

He was born James Travis Reeves in 1924 in Panola County, Texas, and was just ten months old when his father died, leaving his mother to raise him and eight older siblings.

A promising minor-league baseball career was cut short by injury, and Reeves moved into radio announcing. He dabbled in performing while working in Texas in the early 1950s, and in 1953 had an unexpected number-one success with "Mexican Joe," recorded on the Abbott Records label. Reeves's bosses at KWKH in Shreveport,

Above: *Jim Reeves gets it on tape at the RCA studios; visible behind the glass is producer Chet Atkins.* Below: *Reeves in 1954, when he was still a deejay in Shreveport, Louisiana.*

Louisiana, quickly installed him as a member of the *Louisiana Hayride*, which was broadcast from the station.

After two years and several hits later, Reeves landed a contract with RCA Records. He moved to Nashville, and when Chet Atkins encouraged him to lower his voice, the results were two of Reeves's best-known songs, "Four Walls" and "He'll Have to Go."

The singer toured Europe and Africa in 1962, initiating a following that later led to his status as one of country music's most successful international recording stars. In July of 1964, as Reeves was enjoying his thirty-third Top 10 hit, he was killed in the crash of a private plane in a thunderstorm just outside of Nashville. So great was his popularity, however, that he notched 17 posthumous Top 10 hits, including five number-one records and a cleverly engineered 1981 duet with another deceased star, Patsy Cline.

JIM REEVES

Real name: James Travis Reeves
Born: August 20, 1924; Panola County, Texas
Died: July 31, 1964; Nashville, Tennessee
First hit: "Mexican Joe" (1953)
Other notable hits: "Bimbo" (1954), "Four Walls" (1957), "Billy Bayou" (1959), "He'll Have to Go" (1960), "I Guess I'm Crazy" (1964), "Is It Really Over?" (1965)
Awards and achievements: Grand Ole Opry member (1955), Country Music Hall of Fame (1967), 52 Top 10 hits (1953-1982)

Modest and unassuming, Kitty Wells celebrates her arrival at the Grand Ole Opry in 1952 with Roy Acuff (left) and touring partners Johnny Wright (Wells's husband, standing next to her) and Jack Anglin. Wells was to remain a dominant force on country-music charts for more than 15 years.

Kitty Wells is a modest, staunchly traditional woman who would never describe herself as a feminist or a crusader. But by becoming country music's first major female solo star, Wells is regarded as an influential idol whose success helped to open the door for more women performers in a male-dominated field.

One of the few country music stars actually born and reared in Nashville, Wells came into the world on August 30, 1919. Her real name is Muriel Deason; her stage name is an invention of her husband, Johnny Wright, who took the name from an old folk song, "Sweet Kitty Wells." Wells grew up in a fundamentally religious family, and began singing in church early in her life. At age 14, she learned to play acoustic guitar so she could accompany herself while performing hymns on Sunday and Wednesday nights.

She was 16 when she met Wright, who also was interested in music. When Wright auditioned for a job performing on Nashville radio station WSIX, he took Wells and his sister along with him as harmony singers. The trio took their first job singing country music on the station in 1936. A year later, Wright and Wells married. In 1939 Wright hooked up with singer Jack Anglin, forming the duo Johnnie and Jack. Wells joined the two on the road as their "girl singer," a familiar role in many touring bands of the time. Wells helped out with harmonies and performed a few songs of her own during the group's shows.

In 1948, Wells joined the *Louisiana Hayride* with Johnnie and Jack. A beneficiary of the group's spreading fame, Wells signed a solo contract with RCA Records. But her songs received scant attention on country radio and Wells continued to be known primarily as a subordinate member of Johnnie and Jack.

In 1952, however, Wells switched to Decca Records, where company president Paul Cohen suggested she work with Owen Bradley, a producer whose credits included records by Decca's biggest stars, Ernest Tubb and Red Foley. Wells's first single on Decca was a song written in response to Hank Thompson's "The Wild Side of Life," which opened with the line "I didn't know God made honky tonk angels."

Wells's song, "It Wasn't God Who Made Honky Tonk Angels," emphasized male culpability in illicit romances, and became the first by a woman performer to reach the number one position on *Billboard* magazine since the trade sheet initiated the country music charts in 1944. The record spent six weeks at number one and sold more than 800,000 copies. It also introduced Wells's plaintive, unpretentious voice to a large audience. While the song was perched at number one, Wells, Wright, and Anglin were invited to join the Grand Ole Opry.

Wells, a Nashville native, began performing on WSIX radio in 1936, when she was just 16 years old. Earlier that same year she had met singer Johnny Wright, whom she married in 1937.

Following "It Wasn't God Who Made Honky Tonk Angels," Wells continued to record songs that responded to assertions made in hit songs by men. Her second hit, "Paying for That Back Street Affair," followed Webb Pierce's smash "Back Street Affair." Then came "Hey Joe," which provided a feminine answer to Carl Smith's hit of the same name.

From then on, though, Wells's hits stood on their own merits. These were songs of love, anguish, and quiet resignation, and they competed on the charts with releases of male stars in a way no other female singer equalled until Loretta Lynn began hitting the top of the charts in the mid-1960s.

Wells scored 35 Top 10 hits from 1952 to 1965, including such landmark country songs as "Cheatin's a Sin," "Release Me," "Makin' Believe," "Searching (For Someone Like You)," "I Can't Stop Loving You," "Mommy for a Day," "Amigo's Guitar,"

CLASSICS: THE 1940s AND 1950s

Opposite: *Wells helped advance the commercial possibility of women as country music soloists by presenting herself as a wholesome family woman whose songs chastised unfaithful men and handled heartbreak with quiet dignity.* Right: *Many female country music stars regard Wells— who maintained an ambitious touring schedule into the 1990s—as a heroic figure and a major influence.*

"Heartbreak U.S.A.," and "Will Your Lawyer Talk to God." She also was a frequent presence on country radio as a duet performer, attaining hits with Red Foley, Webb Pierce, and Roy Drusky.

In recent years, Wells has accepted praise for her pioneering role with modesty and gracious dignity. She's also quick to point out that she doesn't consider herself an early representative of women's liberation. Her songs and image, she will assert, exemplified her wholesome lifestyle, her religious beliefs, and her opinions about domesticity and family life. As she expressed it in 1988, "In my way of thinking, women are supposed to be the weaker sex and men are supposed to take care of them."

Ultimately, it is the quality of Wells's music and her commercial success that matter most. The course of her career suggested to record companies and radio stations that country music fans were ready to embrace female solo performers. Most of the other successful women country singers of the 1950s performed either with their families or as part of a group, as was the case with Wilma Lee Cooper, Molly O'Day, Rose Maddox, June and Anita Carter, Martha Carson, and Texas Ruby. Although Wells did not always perform alone, her solo career was a milestone in the evolution of

country music. By the early 1960s, a singer like Patsy Cline could flaunt a self-assured independence and record songs that revealed the emotions of a woman in American culture. Then Loretta Lynn, Dolly Parton, Dottie West, and Tammy Wynette more fully explored the female experience in songs they often wrote themselves.

By 1973, Wells had released 461 singles and 43 albums. Though she fell out of favor with radio programmers by the mid-1960s, she has continued to perform regularly and was still averaging more than 100 concerts a year in the 1990s. She was elected into the Country Music Hall of Fame in 1976 and was given a Lifetime Achievement Award by the National Academy of Recording Arts and Sciences in 1991.

KITTY WELLS

Real name: Muriel Deason

Born: August 30, 1919; Nashville, Tennessee

First hit: "It Wasn't God Who Made Honky Tonk Angels" (1952)

Other notable hits: "Release Me" (1954), "Makin' Believe" (1955), "Searching (For Someone Like You)" (1956), "I Can't Stop Loving You" (1959), "Amigo's Guitar" (1960), "Heartbreak U.S.A." (1961)

Awards and achievements: First woman to have number one country song (1952); Grand Ole Opry member (1952); Country Music Hall of Fame (1976); National Academy of Recording Arts and Sciences (NARAS) Lifetime Achievement Award (1991)

RED FOLEY

ed Foley applied his warm baritone to a wide variety of country music, achieving hits with pop-tinged tunes ("Chattanoogie Shoe Shine Boy"), gospel-derived music ("Peace in the Valley for Me"), and high melodrama ("Old Shep"). He also proved adept at hosting radio and television programs, which helped spread the success of country music in the late 1940s and early 1950s.

Clyde Julian Foley was born in 1910 in Blue Lick, Kentucky. His shock of red hair gave him his nickname, and he took to music as a precocious child who quickly learned to play the guitar and harmonica. He won a statewide talent contest at age 17 and was performing in Chicago by the mid-1930s. In 1937, he returned to his native state to start the *Renfro Valley Barn Dance* with radio station owner John Lair.

Two years later, Foley became the first country music artist to host a national network radio show, a program called *Avalon Time*; Foley's co-star was comedian Red Skelton.

In the mid-1940s, Foley became the earliest nationally known performer to record in Nashville. He enjoyed his greatest recording success late in the decade, scoring five Top 10 songs in 1949 and twelve in 1950. Throughout his career, Foley sold more than 24 million records. His fame increased when he hosted ABC-TV's *Ozark Jubilee* show from 1955 to 1961.

Foley was elected into the Country Music Hall of Fame in 1967 and continued to perform until his death a year later.

RED FOLEY

Real name: Clyde Julian Foley
Born: June 17, 1910; Blue Lick, Kentucky
Died: September 19, 1968; Fort Wayne, Indiana
First hit: "Smoke on the Water" (1944)
Other notable hits: "Tennessee Saturday Night" (1949), "Chattanoogie Shoe Shine Boy" (1950), "Just a Closer Walk with Thee" (1950), "Peace in the Valley for Me" (1951), "Alabama Jubilee" (1951), "Midnight" (1953)
Awards and achievements: Cofounded *Renfro Valley Barn Dance*; Grand Ole Opry member (1946-1954); host, *Ozark Jubilee*, ABC-TV (1955-1961); costar, *Mr. Smith Goes to Washington*, ABC-TV (1962); Country Music Hall of Fame (1967)

Above: *Red Foley was a favorite duet partner of many country singers, including Kitty Wells, pictured with Foley in this 1953 recording session.* Below: *Although Foley began as a hillbilly performer, he had matured into a mellow, pop-influenced vocalist by the late 1940s.*

THE LOUVIN BROTHERS

The Louvin Brothers performed chillingly powerful, old-time mountain music at a time when commercial country tunes were moving toward harder-edged honky-tonk and smooth pop. Though considered anachronistic by some of their contemporaries, Ira and Charlie Louvin have continued to grow in stature over the years. Their emotionally stirring high harmonies, sparse instrumental blend, and reverent lyrical style are now considered timeless examples of pure, traditional country music at its best.

The brothers' family name is Loudermilk; Ira was born in 1924, and Charlie followed three years later. They grew up in the small town of Henegar in Northeast Alabama, and their first professional work came in 1943 following a first-place finish in a talent contest in Chattanooga, Tennessee.

World War II briefly interrupted their partnership, but the two reunited in Memphis, where they performed gospel music at a local radio station. In 1949, their only Decca single was released. War separated the brothers for a second time when Charlie went to fight in Korea. Shortly after his return, the Louvins hooked up with MGM Records, where they recorded for a short time before moving on to Capitol in 1952. The brothers released their first big hit, "When I Stop Dreaming," in 1955 and joined the Grand Ole Opry the same year.

The Louvins continued to chart hits through 1962, though their popularity had slipped prior to the start of the new decade. In 1963, they decided to split and pursue solo careers. Ira was killed in an auto accident in 1965; Charlie continues to perform as a member of the Grand Ole Opry.

Charlie (left) and Ira Louvin flank one of their idols, Roy Acuff, in the early 1950s. The brothers' emotional music has proved highly influential.

THE LOUVIN BROTHERS

Real names: Ira Loudermilk; Charles Loudermilk

Born: (Ira) April 24, 1924; Rainesville, Alabama
(Charlie) July 7, 1927; Rainesville, Alabama

Died: (Ira) June 20, 1965; Jefferson City, Missouri

First hit: "When I Stop Dreaming" (1955)

Other notable hits: "I Don't Believe You've Met My Baby" (1956), "Hoping That You're Hoping" (1956), "You're Running Wild" (1956), "Cash on the Barrel Head" (1956), "My Baby's Gone" (1959), "Knoxville Girl" (1959)

Awards and achievements: Grand Ole Opry members (1955-57); nominated for Country Music Hall of Fame

Early in his career Hank Snow modeled himself on Jimmie Rodgers. Soon, though, Snow's mellow, resonant baritone set him on his own path.

Though Hank Snow was closing in on 40 years of age when he achieved his first big country music hit, he nonetheless fashioned one of the longest-running careers of any popular music performer. He also has displayed an ability to create memorable music in a variety of styles, ranging from the insistent boogie of "I'm Movin' On" to the tender sentiment of "(Now and Then, There's) A Fool Such as I" to the western lilt of "Yellow Roses."

He was born Clarence Eugene Snow in 1914 in the Canadian province of Nova Scotia. His parents divorced when he was eight years old and Snow spent a few troubled years with his grandparents. He frequently ran away from home, resulting in his moving in with his mother and her new husband. His stepfather beat him brutally and regularly, and by age 12 Snow ran away for good to join the Merchant Marine as a cabin boy.

While at sea, Snow broke the boredom by learning to play the harmonica. He heard Jimmie Rodgers at age 16 and after raising $30 by unloading salt from a freighter, he bought his first guitar.

Snow imitated Rodgers in his early years, billing himself as "Hank, the Yodeling Ranger." At age 22, he gained his first recording contract with RCA Records in Canada. Nine years later, determined to crack into the U.S. music market, he began traveling across the border into the States. In 1945 he found regular work performing on a radio station in Wheeling, West Virginia. After six months and very little success, Snow headed back to Canada. He spent the next several years living off and on in Hollywood.

In 1949, Snow finally convinced RCA Records to give him a chance in the United States. That same year, he met Ernest Tubb, who convinced the Grand Ole Opry to hire the Canadian. Snow had already changed his billing to "the Singing Ranger" by then, and shortly after joining the Opry he enjoyed his first number-one hit, the smash "I'm Movin' On," which spent 21 weeks at the pole position of the country charts.

Snow quickly piled up a stack of similarly memorable songs, and his resonant baritone brought authority to uptempo country boogies and a gentle wistfulness to ballads. He also was an accomplished guitarist and the first to record an instrumental duet with Chet Atkins.

Snow went on to record 36 Top 10 songs in the 15 years following his first hit, and he continued to hit the number one position as late as 1974. Snow was inducted into the Country Music Hall of Fame in 1979.

HANK SNOW

Real name: Clarence Eugene Snow

Born: May 9, 1914; Liverpool, Nova Scotia, Canada

First hit: "I'm Movin' On" (1950)

Other notable hits: "The Golden Rocket" (1951), "Rhumba Boogie" (1951), "(Now and Then, There's) A Fool Such as I" (1953), "I Don't Hurt Anymore" (1954), "I've Been Everywhere" (1962), "Ninety Miles an Hour (Down a Dead End Street)" (1963)

Awards and achievements: Grand Ole Opry member (1950); Country Music Hall of Fame (1979); 36 Top 10 hits (1950-1974)

Above: *Snow has worked in fast-paced boogie beats and in a sparse, laid-back style that shows off his skillful guitar playing.* Opposite: *Resplendent in a wide variety of custom-made outfits, Snow has been one of country music's most colorful dressers.*

Marty Robbins mastered a variety of musical styles, ranging from cowboy ballads to Hawaiian love songs to rockabilly. His sincerity, talent, and charisma helped him maintain his audience as he skipped across musical influences.

his grandfather was a storyteller and a traveling barker with a medicine show who collected and performed old cowboy songs.

Like many youngsters his age, the young Robbins became enthralled with Gene Autry and other cowboy movie stars. He later told stories of picking cotton all day to make enough money to pay to see an Autry picture on the weekend.

At age 18, he joined the Navy, where he learned guitar and began to appreciate the country music performed by sailors from the South. When he returned home, he began performing in Phoenix nightclubs, changing his name to hide his musical activity from his mother. Soon he began hosting a radio show. One of his guests, Grand Ole Opry star Little Jimmie Dickens, praised his voice and recommended him to Columbia

Robbins joined the Grand Ole Opry in 1953. A fan favorite, he often requested to be the program's final performer, so he could keep singing for the crowd after the radio broadcast ended.

Marty Robbins paid little attention to musical formulas or boundaries. His clear, romantic, mellifluous voice proved flexible enough to encompass everything from traditional cowboy ballads ("El Paso") to teen-oriented pop ("A White Sport Coat and a Pink Carnation") to middle-of-the-road balladry ("My Woman, My Woman, My Wife"), and his wide range helped him enjoy one of country music's longest-spanning careers.

The western lore that was part of Robbins's image came naturally to the native of Glendale, Arizona, where he was born in 1925 and christened Martin David Robinson. His father played harmonica, and

Robbins was fascinated with film and videotape, and left a wealth of footage of his performances in concert and in various cowboy skits and movies. His music and persona thus remain widely accessible.

Records in Nashville. Robbins was signed and his first Columbia single, "I'll Go On Alone," spent two weeks at number one early in 1953. He joined the Opry cast a few months later, but didn't achieve a second number-one record for three years, when a change in direction led to the rock-influenced hit, "Singin' the Blues."

Robbins spent the end of the 1950s directing songs toward the burgeoning teen market. Then in 1959 a shift in style led to another enormous hit, the great Spanish-influenced cowboy story ballad, "El Paso." He went on to star in 18 low-budget westerns, including the classic *Ballad of a Gunfighter* in 1963.

Robbins maintained a high profile on the charts in his second and third decades as a performer, achieving 17 Top 10 hits in the 1960s and 15 more in the 1970s. He also led a colorful, adventurous private life: An interest in stock car racing resulted in his earning a berth in the competitive NASCAR circuit until a series of serious accidents convinced him to give up participation in the sport. He suffered a heart attack in 1969 and became the fifteenth person to undergo a bypass operation.

Robbins was inducted into the Country Music Hall of Fame in October 1982. Two months later, on December 8, he died of a heart attack.

MARTY ROBBINS

Real name: Martin David Robinson

Born: September 26, 1925; Glendale, Arizona

Died: December 8, 1982; Nashville, Tennessee

First hit: "I'll Go On Alone" (1953)

Other notable hits: "Singin' the Blues" (1956), "A White Sport Coat" (1957), "El Paso" (1959), "Don't Worry" (1961), "Devil Woman" (1962), "My Woman, My Woman, My Wife" (1970), "El Paso City" (1976)

Awards and achievements: Grand Ole Opry member (1953); Country Music Hall of Fame (1982); Grammy Award, Best Country Vocal, Male (1959, 1970)

JOHNNY CASH

Left: *Country music's most visible male star is Johnny Cash, captured here in a pensive mood in Nashville in 1962.* Opposite: *Despite the monumental popularity that has sold countless records and filled numberless live venues, Cash has continued to choose material that reflects the concerns of the common man.*

families to productive land. The farm was located in a remote region, and the family home didn't receive electricity until 1946. By then, one of Cash's brothers had died.

The Cash family entertained themselves with music, with everyone joining in on traditional gospel and old country songs, including a heavy dose of Carter Family tunes. Johnny began writing songs by the time he reached high school.

After graduation, Cash moved to Pontiac, Michigan, to work in a Fisher Body Plant. Eventually worn down by boredom, he joined the U.S. Air Force and spent four years in Germany. While there, he taught himself to play guitar. His first performances were for crowds of soldiers on foreign military bases.

When he returned, he settled in Memphis. He had met his first wife, Vivian, while in the Air Force. He also met two musicians, guitarist Luther Perkins and bassist Marshall Grant, and began performing informally with them. He talked them into auditioning at Sun Records, home of Elvis Presley and Carl Perkins. Their first song was "Hey Porter." Sun owner Sam Phillips was intrigued, and asked Cash to come up with something with more of a rock beat. The singer went home and wrote "Cry,

Johnny Cash is the most internationally recognized figure in country music. The Man In Black has secured more pop hits than any other country artist; and only Eddy Arnold and George Jones have enjoyed more country music chart hits. Cash has been a movie actor, a best-selling author, and a host of a successful TV series. He counts among his friends such diverse people as Billy Graham, Mick Jagger, Richard Nixon, and Bob Dylan. He writes from the point of view of the common man, yet he's sat across the table from kings.

Cash was born on February 26, 1932, into a impoverished farm family in Kingsland, Arkansas. He was three years old when his parents, Ray and Carrie Cash, bought 20 acres of cotton fields near Dyess, Arkansas, with help from a government New Deal program that relocated farm

CLASSICS: THE 1940s AND 1950s

Cash (center) leads friend and fellow country singer Johnny Horton (right) on a tour of Dyess, Arkansas. No stranger to the harsh side of life, Cash was three years old when his father bought 20 acres near Dyess to farm cotton.

Cry, Cry," which became his first country music hit in 1955 as recorded by Johnny Cash and the Tennessee Two. (Several years later, when drummer Fluke Holland joined, they became the Tennessee Three.)

Those initial songs featured the singular Cash sound: A walking bass and a simple, deep-toned, single-note guitar provided primitive backing. In search of a stark sound, Cash purposely omitted the fiddles and steel guitars that rang out on most country music of the period. Cash's music focused attention on the singer's foreboding, earthy voice, a baritone so ominous and penetrating that it

demanded attention despite its limited range.

Within his first year at Sun, Cash released two of his most famous songs, "Folsom Prison Blues" and "I Walk the Line." The latter became his first number-one country hit, as well as his initial major pop hit, reaching number 17 on the *Billboard* charts. It has since been recorded by more than 100 artists.

In 1956, Cash became the first Sun Records artist to join the Grand Ole Opry. Two years later, he signed with Columbia Records. His second Columbia single, "Don't Take Your Guns to Town," sold a half-million copies

and continued Cash's run of success on both the country and pop charts.

In the 1960s, while recording a series of folk-influenced albums on such themes as the plight of the American Indians and the romance of trains, Cash descended into a well-documented period of drug use. By his own account, he cleaned himself up with the support of singer June Carter, becoming a born-again Christian along the way. The couple married in 1968. That same year, Cash achieved his first number-one hit in four years with a live version of "Folsom Prison Blues," recorded during a historic concert at the

After recovering from heart surgery in 1989, Cash returned to performing across the United States and in frequent tours of Europe, where he is immensely popular.

Rising," "Don't Take Your Guns to Town," "I Still Miss Someone," "Understand Your Man," and "Get Rhythm." His autobiography, *The Man In Black*, has sold more than 1.4 million copies. His novel, *Man In White*, about the conversion of the Apostle Paul, also reached the best-seller lists.

In 1980, Cash became the youngest person inducted into the Country Music Hall of Fame.

In 1986, Cash was let go after 28 years with Columbia Records. Although the dismissal created an immediate uproar within the Nashville music community, Cash responded humbly, accepting a new contract with Mercury Records.

The legendary singer underwent heart bypass surgery in February 1989, but by the spring of that year he was performing regularly again. In 1992, he continued to record for Mercury Records and maintained a heavy touring schedule.

California prison named in the song.

His new bride and her mother, country star Maybelle Carter, were regular guests on the ABC-TV series *The Johnny Cash Show*, which ran from 1969 to 1971. That led to a career revival that resulted in 11 Top Five songs during the years the show was on the air.

The statistics compiled by Cash during his career are staggering. He has sold more than 50 million records. He has won seven Grammy Awards. He has put 48 singles on the pop charts and more than 130 songs on the country charts.

His recognition as a writer is similarly impressive. He's received 23 citations from the song-tracking agency BMI for radio airplay received by such classic songs as "Folsom Prison Blues," "I Walk the Line," "Big River," "I Got Stripes," "Five Feet High and

JOHNNY CASH

Real name: John R. Cash

Born: February 26, 1932; Kingsland, Arkansas

First hit: "Cry, Cry, Cry" (1955)

Other notable hits: "Folsom Prison Blues" (1956/1968), "I Walk the Line" (1956), "Guess Things Happen That Way" (1958), "Don't Take Your Guns to Town" (1959), "Ring of Fire" (1963), "A Boy Named Sue" (1969)

Awards and achievements: Youngest person inducted into Country Music Hall of Fame (1980); 50 million records sold; 48 pop hits (1955-1976); 132 country hits (1955-1988); 23 Broadcast Music, Inc. (BMI) songwriting citations

THE NEXT GENERATION: THE 1960s AND 1970s

L̲ike a pair of faithful blue jeans, the Nashville Sound started to come apart at its Southern seams in the 1960s and '70s.

The Nashville Sound—resplendent in maudlin tales of young love, old dogs, and other homespun images—had been delivered for 50 years with a rigid rural resonance characterized by bluesy Southern playing and lavish, formulated arrangements.

Television's Hee Haw *brought country music to a mass audience on a scale that had never been achieved before. The show was unsophisticated, to be sure, but it did bring the country sound into millions of American homes. Seen here are stars Grandpa Jones (far left) and Roy Clark (center), in a number with guest Barbara Mandrell.*

But by the early sixties country stars of the fifties began to age and their star power diminished. Traditionalism began to crack beneath the strain of the passing years. Just as significant, the business end of popular music blossomed in the sixties and seventies; Nashville could no longer afford to distance itself from other musical influences, particularly rock 'n' roll.

In response, country music sought out new, non-traditional audiences. In 1962, Patsy Cline became the first country star to appear in Las Vegas, in a two-week booking at the Mint Lounge. Marty Robbins followed her to the gambling city in 1963. Today, country music can be enjoyed up and down the Vegas strip.

Television affected every aspect of popular culture in the sixties and country music was not shy about getting involved. *The Johnny Cash Show* aired on ABC from 1969 to 1971; at the same time on CBS, Buck Owens and Roy Clark headed the ensemble cast of *Hee Haw*, which was a country version of NBC's irreverent *Rowan and Martin's Laugh-In* comedy series. *Hee Haw* lasted just two seasons on CBS, but enjoyed a wildly successful rebirth after segueing into syndication in 1971. Although the show trafficked in hillbilly imagery and cornball humor, it nevertheless brought country music to a mass audience.

The success of country music on the small screen gave sudden credence to a new style of performer—"crossover" country artists like Glen Campbell and Kenny Rogers, who used country-music sentiments and conventions as a springboard for a more accessible, country-pop sound.

A particularly direct response to television's easygoing interpretation of country was the so-called outlaw movement, which began in 1973 when Waylon Jennings recorded *Honky Tonk Heroes*, an album of stark, uncompromising songs by Texas songwriter Billy Joe Shaver. Then, in 1976, Willie Nelson hit the outlaw trail with a take-no-

Las Vegas (above), *long a refuge for pop-oriented "lounge singers," opened its doors to country artists in the 1960s, many of whom enjoyed considerable success. One of the beneficiaries was pop-country singer Glen Campbell* (right), *who exemplified the pleasant but innocuous "crossover" sound.*

prisoners cover of Lefty Frizzell's "If You've Got the Money, I've Got the Time" at the Country Music Association awards show.

Country's collective jaw dropped.

The mixture of outlaw, non-traditionalist, and crossover artists overshadowed the once-glittering legends of Chet Atkins, Patsy Cline, Merle Haggard, and George Jones, all of whom had been at their commercial peak in the early sixties.

Gram Parsons (top, left) fronted the innovative Flying Burrito Brothers.

By the end of the seventies the old-liners had fallen out of fashion, but they each had at least one identifiable musical descendant. Perhaps the most important of these latter-day, country-influenced artists was Bob Dylan. Typed early in his career as a "folk-protest" singer, Dylan listened to the tense, authoritative vocals of George Jones, proceeded to put his own unique spin on the music, and sparked an entirely new musical subcategory: country-rock. Dylan's 1966 double album *Blonde on Blonde* and 1969's *Nashville Skyline* were both recorded in Nashville, and were enormously exciting comminglings of rock and country music. In *Blonde on Blonde*, for instance, Dylan introduced assertive rock guitar and prodigious keyboards to the Nashville studio scene while using traditional session men like Charlie McCoy and Hargus Robbins.

Dylan's innovations helped take the twang out of country and established a wide-open landscape for country-rock bands such as the Flying Burrito Brothers, who debuted in 1969 with bassist Chris Hillman and vocalist Gram Parsons, formerly of the Southern California folk-rock group the Byrds. Suddenly, new country artists were coming from everywhere.

Left, above: *Bob Dylan's* Nashville Skyline *energized country music as well as rock 'n' roll when it appeared in 1969. Four years later, Waylon Jennings's* Honky Tonk Heroes (left) *mated a hard-edged contemporary sound with honky-tonk sentiments. Together, these albums opened exciting — and quite divergent—avenues for country music.*

So it was that the stage was set for country music's biggest commercial explosion since The Nashville Sound—a fresh, accessible style created by a new breed of stars who not only incorporated rock 'n' roll musical influences, but also used rock 'n' roll themes, theatrics, and venues to reach larger numbers of people.

Country music had always celebrated the past.

Throughout the 1960s and '70s, it laid the foundation that would eventually enable it to confront the future.

Traditional to his core, George Jones maintained a firm grip on his audience in the sixties and seventies. Possessed of a remarkably evocative vocal style, he influenced Bob Dylan and, indirectly, helped chart the course of the new country music in those decades.

PATSY CLINE

Patsy Cline is an everlasting echo of the Nashville Sound. The Nashville Sound was shaped in the 1950s as the industry's response to rebel rockabilly. Although younger listeners favored rockabilly's hard-pedal steel set against piercing harmony, the Nashville Sound was a more comfortable style of sweeping strings and dramatic backing choirs. The even temperament of Cline's vocals was a perfect conduit for the Nashville Sound. Cline's music endures today because of her ability to balance country sentiment with pop charms.

Patsy Cline was born Virginia Patterson Hensley on September 8, 1932, in Gore, Virginia. Her family moved about 15 miles away to Winchester when she was in grammar school. Cline was a wunderkind, winning a tap-dancing contest at the age of four and learning to play the piano at eight. One of her earliest vocal experiences was singing duets with her mother at the Gore Baptist Church.

She was first noticed by a member of a Grand Ole Opry country music show touring troupe who stopped in Winchester when she was 16. Cline auditioned and won a guest spot on the local billing. Following a suggestion that she audition for the Opry, Patsy made the trip to Nashville. But when doors didn't open immediately, finances forced her to return home a few days later.

In the early 1950s, a bandleader suggested she come up with a more country-sounding first name. She adapted her middle name to Patsy and took the last name of Gerald Cline, to whom she was married between 1952 and 1957.

As Patsy Cline, she was signed by Four Star Records in 1954. A distribution deal with Decca led in 1955 to her first recordings under Nashville vocal producer Owen Bradley, who had previously brought out the best in Kitty Wells.

Cline's first career break came in January 1957, when she was a winner on the *Arthur Godfrey Talent Scouts* show singing the bluesy "Walkin' After Midnight" and Hank Williams's "Your Cheatin' Heart." Decca Records subsequently released "Walkin' After Midnight" as a single; it became a hit on the country charts and reached number 12 on the pop charts. Ironically, Cline had not wanted to record "Walkin' After Midnight," feeling it was not country enough.

"In the beginning, we were trying to be country like Jean Shepard and Kitty Wells," Owen

THE NEXT GENERATION: THE 1960s AND 1970s

Bradley told *Goldmine* magazine. "If we'd made Patsy Cline in the '50s like we did in the '60s, we wouldn't have survived the '50s! They would have said, 'What are you sending us those Kay Starr records, or those pop records, for?' See, they would have been so much like pop records, they would have said, 'You're the country department. If you're going to make pop records, either come up here or you're fired.'"

Later in 1957 Patsy divorced Gerald Cline and married Charlie Dick. Academy-Award-winning actress Jessica Lange portrayed Cline in the biographical 1985 movie *Sweet Dreams*. In 1991 Lange told the Associated Press, "Patsy didn't hold anything back. If her husband is late for a dinner she had fussed over, she lets him know it, and the scene erupts into an explosive argument. She had a way of hitting life head-on." That carried over into Cline's music, whether it was a purposefully distant cover of Hank Williams's "Your Cheatin' Heart" or the liberated send-off on "Imagine That."

At first glance the five-foot-six-inch, brown-eyed Cline might have seemed innocent. Her hobbies included collecting salt and pepper shakers and collecting pictures of country-western stars. But when it came to making music, Cline had a strong will.

Because of Cline's country convictions, she found it difficult to follow up the immediate crossover success of "Walkin' After Midnight." Decca then eliminated fiddles and steel guitar in favor of polish and backing vocals.

On August 25, 1958, Cline gave birth to Julia Simadore Dick. Cline didn't return to the pop charts

Since Cline's death in 1963, her music has grown in popularity, making her one of the best-selling artists in the history of MCA Records. Her Greatest Hits *album was certified gold in 1985, platinum in 1987, double platinum in 1989, and triple platinum in 1991. Actual sales surpass 3.5 million.*

until 1961, with "I Fall to Pieces" (which was turned down by Roy Drusky, among others) and Willie Nelson's honky-tonk composition "Crazy," which cracked the Top 10 in pop.

By this time Cline's voice had developed a stunning sophistication that mixed with the understated commercial charm of Patti Page. Page had taken country to pop as early as 1950 by selling five million copies of Pee Wee King's country tune "Tennessee Waltz." And in 1952 Page recorded the wanderlust ballad "You Belong to Me," which became a pop hit. Cline recorded

the same song for a country audience in 1962.

Cline had other country hits in 1962, including Harlan Howard's "When I Get Through With You (You'll Love Me Too)" and "She's Got You," whose dramatic narrative texture created another pop breakthrough.

On March 5, 1963, one month to the day after she recorded "Sweet Dreams (Of You)," Cline was killed in a plane crash. She had performed at a benefit in Kansas City, Kansas, the night before. Along with fellow country stars Lloyd "Cowboy" Copas and

Hawkshaw Hawkins, Cline was flying back to Nashville in a private plane piloted by her manager. After a refueling stop in Dyersberg, Tennessee, the plane encountered bad weather and crashed, killing all aboard.

Cline's music grew in popularity after her death. Album sales averaged 75,000 per year through the 1960s and 1970s. Sales increased even more after her role in Loretta Lynn's career was dramatized in the 1980 movie *Coal Miner's Daughter*. Cline and Lynn had been close friends.

When Cline died, she and Kitty Wells were the top women stars in country music. Loretta Lynn's career was just beginning. Tammy Wynette and Dolly Parton were waiting in the wings.

Cline was elected to the Country Music Hall of Fame in 1973. She was the first female soloist chosen for the honor.

PATSY CLINE

Real name: Virginia Patterson Hensley

Born: September 8, 1932; Gore, Virginia

Died: March 5, 1963; Camden, Texas

First hit: "Walkin' After Midnight" (1957)

Other notable hits: "I Fall to Pieces" (1961), "Crazy" (1961), "She's Got You" (1962), "When I Get Through With You (You'll Love Me Too)" (1962), "Sweet Dreams (Of You)" (1963)

Awards and achievements: Grand Ole Opry member (1960), Country Music Hall of Fame (1973); *Greatest Hits* album certified triple platinum (1991); Recording Academy Hall of Fame (1992)

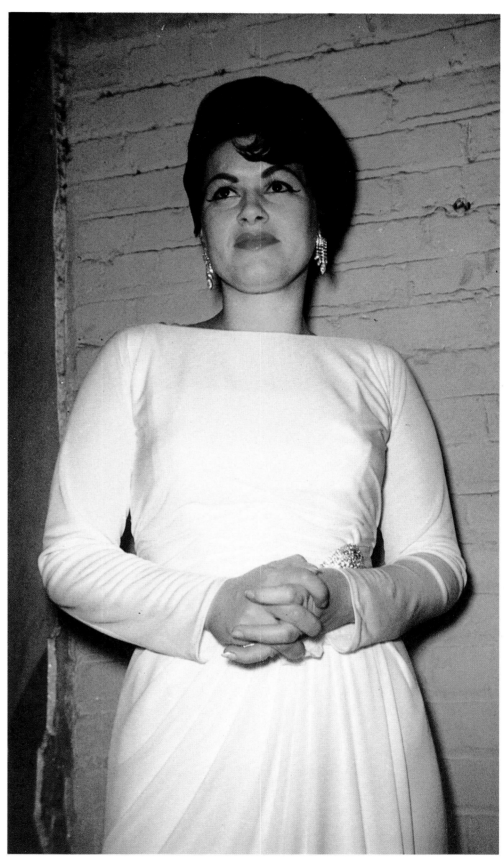

Cline backstage at her final concert, a March 4, 1963, benefit for disc jockey Cactus Jack Call in Kansas City, Kansas. Patsy's death the following day did not end her recording career: She had a new hit as late as 1981, when her producer, Owen Bradley, electronically paired her voice with that of the late Jim Reeves to create a hit duet, "Have You Ever Been Lonely."

Always an innovator, Chet Atkins insists that his guitars be designed and adapted to his standards. He began designing guitars in 1955, when he created a series of signature models for the Gretsch Guitar Company.

If the Nashville Sound was constructed around accessible voices like those of Patsy Cline, Jim Reeves, and Conway Twitty, then Chet Atkins was the commercial architect. It was Atkins who removed the traditional steel guitar and fiddle from the records he produced for RCA in the late 1950s and early 1960s.

"All I did was try and sell records," Atkins told the Chicago *Sun-Times* in a 1985 interview. "I found you had to surprise friends and neighbors with every release. You had to have something different in it."

Atkins thought the deep country sound of traditional instrumentation limited country music's potential for radio airplay. As American families migrated to the cities, country audiences became less traditional in their listening habits. Atkins's "countrypolitan" strings-and-horns stylings can be heard on the early recordings of Reeves, Skeeter Davis, and Bobby Bare.

Atkins was born on June 20, 1924, in Luttrell, Tennessee, near Knoxville. He grew up in an intense musical environment. Atkins's father was a piano and voice teacher, and Atkins was exposed to such country legends as Jimmie Rodgers as early as three years of age.

The first instrument Atkins played was the fiddle; he didn't pick up the guitar until the ripe old age of nine. Atkins is a pioneer of the Southern thumb-and-finger picking technique in which the thumb plays bass notes and keeps time while the fingers play the melody.

Atkins is regarded as the most recorded instrumental soloist of all time. In the late 1940s he played guitar and fiddle behind Red Foley, the Carter Sisters, and Mother Maybelle. By 1950 he had become the top session guitarist in Nashville.

Atkins joined the Grand Ole Opry in 1950. He was inducted into the Country Music Hall of Fame in 1973. Atkins has won nine Country Music Association Awards and ten Grammys. He has sold more than 30 million records.

Atkins keeps a contemporary pace, and he hasn't confined his career to country music. He has performed with Arthur Fiedler and the Boston Pops, jazz-pop musician George Benson, and Indian sitarist Ravi Shankar. And early in 1990 Atkins recorded *Neck and Neck* with Mark Knopfler of Dire Straits. It was these challenging affiliations that sparked Atkins's best performances.

Awards and accolades have been deeply appreciated by Atkins, but whenever the subject of the Nashville Sound comes up, he doesn't forget the bottom line. In 1985 he told the Chicago *Sun-Times*: "A friend was with me during an interview a while back and he interrupted, 'I'll tell you exactly what "the Nashville Sound" is,' and he got some money out and jingled it. That's the Nashville Sound."

CHET ATKINS

Real name: Chester Burton Atkins

Born: June 20, 1924; Luttrell, Tennessee

First hit: "Country Gentlemen" (1949)

Other notable hits: "Gallopin' Guitar" (1949), "Main Street Breakdown" (1949), "Yakety Axe" (1965), "Snowbird" (1971), "Fiddlin' Around" (1974), "Poor Boy Blues" (with Mark Knopfler) (1990)

Awards and achievements: Grand Ole Opry member (1950), 10 Grammy awards (1967–1990), Country Music Hall of Fame (1973), nine Country Music Association (CMA) awards (1967-1985), CMA Musician of the Year (1988), more than 75 albums recorded, more than 30 million records sold

---

Opposite: *Porter Wagoner (left) is just one of a legion of Chet Atkins fans; branches of the Chet Atkins Appreciation Society can be found in England, France, and the United States. Fans and guitar students meet annually in Nashville for a four-day convention of guitar seminars that is capped off by an Atkins concert.*

BUCK OWENS

Buck Owens (left) championed a hard-driving beat in country music. In doing so, he helped inspire such latter-day stars as Dwight Yoakam, seen here with Owens in the late 1980s.

my records, they weren't going to buy them anymore. But I felt that's what I needed for my songs."

Owens played saxophone and trumpet as part of the Schoolhouse Playboys' rhythm-soaked shows between 1951 and 1958. The Schoolhouse Playboys were more a rockabilly outfit than a country band, which attracted Owens to the drums.

"As late as 1960, the first time I appeared on the Grand Ole Opry by myself, the only thing they would let me have was a snare drum with no mike," Owens told the *Sun-Times*. "The guy got to stand behind me and play with brushes. They didn't want to be too modern too quick, and I used to beat 'em up about that."

It was Buck Owens who helped introduce arresting percussion to a once-stoic country music form. Owens's elevation of the drum into a position of prominence alongside the steel guitar helped establish open space for the 1980s country rock movement spearheaded by Dwight Yoakam.

Alvis Edgar Owens, Jr., was born August 12, 1929, in Sherman, Texas. His father, a sharecropper, moved the family to Mees, Arizona, when Owens was eight years old. Owens remained in Arizona until he was 22, when he went to Bakersfield, California, to form his first band, the Schoolhouse Playboys.

"Being born in Texas and by being part of the *Grapes of Wrath* migration to California, I was accustomed to dance," Owens told the Chicago *Sun-Times*. "I remember getting letters from people who said since I put a little tom-tom on

Owens is best known to the general public as co-host (with Roy Clark, right) of Hee Haw, *the long-running comedy-variety series. His success on this admittedly cornball program overshadowed the considerable contribution he has made to country music.*

Bakersfield became the perfect environment for experimentalists such as Owens and Merle Haggard. Away from the more manufactured Nashville, their invigorating, jazzy strain of country music became more expressive. And Owens's syrupy tenor would not have sounded as distinguished in polished Nashville.

Owens left the Schoolhouse Playboys in 1957 to replace Ferlin Husky in the Tommy Collins Band in Bakersfield. Signed by Capitol Records as a solo artist in 1957, his first hit, the swaggering "Second Fiddle," danced through country's Top 40 in mid-1959.

In 1962, Owens formed his backup group, the Buckaroos. They had what is probably their best known hit, "I've Got a Tiger by the Tail," in 1965. Between 1969 and 1986, Owens was cohost of *Hee Haw*; his cornball television image has overshadowed his unique musical contributions.

Owens once claimed to have retired, though he was lured back into the studio by singer Dwight Yoakum in 1988; their duet, "Streets of Bakersfield," was a number-one country hit. Still, Owens does not have to work: He has made wise business investments over the years. He owns television and radio stations and several magazines and printing presses. Now he spends his leisure time playing golf and being active in numerous Southern California charity events.

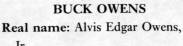

BUCK OWENS
Real name: Alvis Edgar Owens, Jr.
Born: August 12, 1929; Sherman, Texas
First hit: "Second Fiddle" (1959)
Other notable hits: "Under Your Spell Again" (1959), "Excuse Me (I Think I've Got A Heartache)" (1960), "Act Naturally" (1963), "Love's Gonna Live Here" (1963), "I've Got a Tiger by the Tail" (1965), "Streets of Bakersfield" (with Dwight Yoakam, 1988)
Awards and achievements: Grand Ole Opry member (1960); 31 consecutive Top 10 hits (1963-1972); 12 number one albums; Country Music Association (CMA) Instrumental Group of the Year (with the Buckaroos, 1967, 1968); *Billboard* Top Country Male Singles and Albums Artist of the Decade (1969)

Owens put together a remarkable string of hits in the fifties and sixties. He became wealthy and now has many successful business holdings, but it is his direct, urgent music that will be his real legacy.

Loretta Lynn has won more awards from the Country Music Association and the Academy of Country Music than any other female performer. Her resourceful upbringing is a classic country music story.

Sources differ on whether Lynn was born in 1932 or 1935. She was born Loretta Webb on April 14 in Butcher Holler, Kentucky. She grew up in a log cabin in the back hills of Kentucky. Her father was a coal miner, which was the peg of her best-selling 1976 autobiography and the 1980 Academy-Award-winning film, *Coal Miner's Daughter*.

When Webb was 13, she met a 19-year-old boy named O. V. Lynn at a town dance. A month later Loretta and "Mooney," as he was known to friends, had obtained her father's permission to get married—even though his nickname was derived from "Moonshine."

Within a year, Mooney lost his job and hitchhiked to Washington state with Loretta's brother, Jay Lee Webb. Mooney found a job as a Washington logger while Loretta stayed home, pregnant with their first child. Loretta Lynn was 14.

Lynn eventually relocated to Custer, Washington. She helped pay the rent by cooking for 30 farmhands at a nearby ranch. Lynn had four of her six children before she was 21 and was a grandmother at 32.

Mooney bought Lynn a modest Sears guitar for her 18th birthday. She taught herself guitar, and she still cannot read music. On the encouragement of Mooney, she sat in with a local band one Saturday night. She did so well she was asked to become a regular member

The late Marty Robbins is just one of many top country artists who sang duets with Loretta Lynn. The legendary country queen has brought out the best in all of her collaborators.

of the Saturday night review. By the late 1950s Lynn had formed her own band with Jay Lee Webb on guitar, and they traveled around the Northwest. Mooney assumed a greater role in her career and became her manager.

Her first record was a 45, titled "Honky Tonk Girl," inspired by a woman Lynn saw drinking and crying in a Washington tavern. Mooney mailed out 3,000 copies to radio stations across the country. Favorable response gave Lynn the confidence to head toward Nashville, where the record became a small hit. In the fall of 1961, Lynn was signed by Decca Records, and she joined the Grand Ole Opry.

Lynn had a difficult time establishing a musical identity. Her surly country tonality sounded too much like Kitty Wells, whom she emulated in her formative years. Producer Owen Bradley, who had

been instrumental in the development of Patsy Cline, produced Lynn's "Success," her first Decca hit. The ballad features the steel and twin fiddles that had been deemed inappropriate for Cline. Lynn tried to mimic Cline's quivering range, compromising the caustic rural timbre that was to define Lynn's later recordings.

Cline immediately befriended Lynn by lending support to the new girl in town. But with their friendship a little over a year old, Cline died in a plane crash in March 1963.

Lynn's independence resurfaced and she began having hits with her own compositions. Her "Before I'm Over You" made the Top 10 on the country charts in 1963. The follow-up hit was 1964's "Wine, Women and Song." In 1965 she had three Top 10 singles: "Blue Kentucky Girl" (written by Johnny Mullings), "Happy Birthday," and "The Home You're Tearing Down."

An identity was finally being established. Social attitudes were rapidly changing in the mid-1960s. Lynn caught a cultural wave with such tough-talking compositions as "Don't Come Home a-Drinkin' (With Lovin' on Your Mind)" (1966), "Fist City" (1968), and "Your Squaw Is on the Warpath" (1968). More than a couple of these tunes were inspired by Mooney's behavior, who counted Cline's second husband among his drinking buddies.

Opposite: *Sometimes Lynn is most at home outside the home. She and husband Mooney Lynn own more than 100 horses, as well as the entire town of Hurricane Mills, Tennessee, some 65 miles west of Nashville.*

THE NEXT GENERATION: THE 1960s AND 1970s

In 1980 Lynn was named Artist of the Decade 1970-1980 by the Academy of Country Music. Here, she accepts the award, flanked by half-sister Crystal Gayle (right) and her mother, Clara Marie Webb.

Opposite: *Loretta Lynn has led a life that defines the working-class struggles that figure so prominently in country music. Born into poverty, she had four of her six children by the time she was 21. She was 27 when she cut her first record and a grandmother at 32.*

attempting to cross a river near Nashville on horseback. He was 34, the oldest of her six children.

"That's the worst heartache I've ever had," Lynn told *USA Today* in 1991. "I miss him more all the time. I play games that he'll be comin' in. When I come in off the road, sometimes he'd come see me and sometimes he'd be busy. I pretend that he's busy."

Her sassy self-declaration had shaped Lynn into an almost mythical figure. In the '70s she forged ahead with deeply autobiographical songs—"Coal Miner's Daughter" (1970) and the traditional shuffle "You're Lookin' at Country." Lynn showed there was a way out of oppression and poverty.

Lynn also continued a country tradition of male-female duets. Between 1964 and 1969 she dueted with Ernest Tubb, and while their vocals were unsettled and mismatched, the country charm was irresistible. A better match for Lynn's penetrating vocals was the quieter, almost subservient style of country star Conway Twitty. Their most notable tunes were 1971's "After the Fire Is Gone," which won a Grammy Award for best country vocal performance by a duo or group, and 1978's "You're the Reason Our Kids Are Ugly."

Lynn's last statement of impact was "The Pill," a 1975 song about a wife who enjoys the sexual liberation brought on by birth control. Disc jockeys initially refused to play "The Pill." Lynn was fond of saying, "If they'd had the pill when I was having babies, I'd be eatin' them like popcorn."

Lynn will go down in history as the first woman winner of the Country Music Association's Entertainer of the Year award. Lynn was given the award in 1972. In 1988 she was elected to the Country Music Hall of Fame.

In recent years Lynn has slowed down, owing in part to health problems. The marriage with Mooney, however, has remained intact. The Lynns own several houses, including three in Nashville. At one of their Nashville homes, they have built a huge corral for the more than 100 horses they own.

The greatest hardship of Lynn's tumultuous life has been the death of her son, Jack Benny Lynn, who drowned in July 1984 while

LORETTA LYNN

Real name: Loretta Webb

Born: April 14, 1932 or 1935; Butcher Holler, Kentucky

First hit: "Honky Tonk Girl" (1960)

Other notable hits: "Success" (1962), "Before I'm Over You" (1963), "Blue Kentucky Girl" (1965), "The Home You're Tearing Down" (1965), "Your Squaw Is on the Warpath" (1968), "Coal Miner's Daughter" (1970), "The Pill" (1975)

Awards and achievements: Grand Ole Opry member (1961); Country Music Association (CMA) Female Vocalist of the Year (1967, 1972, 1973); Grammy, Best Country Vocal Performance by a Group (with Conway Twitty, 1971); first woman named CMA Entertainer of the Year (1972); American Music Awards Award of Merit (1985); Country Music Hall of Fame (1988); more CMA and Academy of Country Music awards than any other female performer

THE NEXT GENERATION: THE 1960s AND 1970s

MERLE HAGGARD

Merle Haggard is an American original. He carries a proud tradition of singing pro-American songs like "Okie from Muskogee," "The Fighting Side of Me," and "Me and Crippled Soldiers."

Anyone who divides country music into camps of old and new traditions is missing a critical point, one that Merle Haggard has hung his cowboy hat on for his entire career. Haggard's greatest challenge has been to redefine tradition.

"There was always a button," Haggard told the Chicago *Sun-Times.* "It's like jazz players who have this little button if they get too close to the melody, they go in another direction. Well, to tell you the truth, if I felt I was conforming just a little bit, I'd do something wrong. I hated to be someone you could count on to do a certain

thing. I hated to be anticipated, and I didn't realize how important that was to me."

It has worked. Haggard has had 38 number-one country hits, which is more than Hank Williams, Sr., and Johnny Cash combined. Haggard's 1968 confessional "Today I Started Loving You Again" has been covered by more than 400 artists. He has been nominated 43 times for Country Music Association awards—more than any other male country entertainer. Haggard's other hits include 1968's "Mama Tried" and his 1969 signature song "Okie from Muskogee."

Haggard was born on April 6, 1937, in Bakersfield, California. In 1934 his parents spun out of the Dust Bowl in Oklahoma during the Depression and settled in a "Hoover Camp" in Oildale, California, near Bakersfield.

Haggard's father got a low-paying job for the Santa Fe Railroad, which left a lasting impression on Merle. To this day, Haggard travels in a tour bus that carries the Santa Fe logo.

The family was living in a converted boxcar when Haggard was born. His father died when Haggard was nine years old. He grew more rebellious as he got older. He started hopping short-line trains and at the same time first heard the liberating yodel of Jimmie Rodgers.

"When I heard those Jimmie Rodgers songs, I felt it was something I had to do—hop some freights, and unconsciously go to prison, too," Haggard told the *Sun-Times.* "It's almost like there was a certain education I had to come by and certain things to get under my belt."

Between 1957 and 1960 Haggard did time in San Quentin on a second-degree burglary conviction. He repatterned his life in the prison textile mill. Upon his release, Haggard returned to Bakersfield and began playing the country music he had learned in prison.

From the first time Haggard walked on a stage, his style has been impossible to define. Along with the Strangers, his innovative nine-piece band, Haggard has always played a kaleidoscope of pop, swing, blues, and what Haggard terms country jazz.

Left: *Sometimes life has been upside-down for Haggard. He landed in San Quentin prison between 1957 and 1960 for a second-degree burglary conviction. Just a decade after his parole, he was Country Music Association Entertainer of the Year. Below: The face of country music. "The Hag," as Haggard is known, has had 38 number-one country hits—more than Hank Williams and Johnny Cash combined.*

MERLE HAGGARD

Born: April 6, 1937; Bakersfield, California

First hit: "Sing a Sad Song" (1963)

Other notable hits: "All My Friends Are Gonna Be Strangers" (1965), "I'm a Lonesome Fugitive" (1967), "Today I Started Loving You Again" (1968), "Okie From Muskogee" (1969), "If We Make It Through December" (1973), "Big City" (1982)

Awards and achievements: Country Music Association (CMA) Entertainer of the Year (1970); CMA Male Vocalist of the Year (1970); CMA Single of the Year (1970); CMA Album of the Year (1970); CMA Vocal Duo of the Year (with Willie Nelson, 1983); Grammy, Best Country Vocal Performance, Male (1984); 43 CMA award nominations, more than any other country entertainer; 38 number-one singles; four gold albums

TAMMY WYNETTE

Of all the female voices that have crossed country music to pop, none is more manipulative than Tammy Wynette's. Her best-known hits, "Stand By Your Man," "D-I-V-O-R-C-E," and "I Don't Wanna Play House," are characterized by the cries of pedal steel guitars that cling to the pain in her voice. The delicate balance between sublime instrumentation and soft vocals is what shapes Wynette's survivor personality.

Wynette was born Virginia Wynette Pugh on May 5, 1942, in a tar-paper shack on her grandfather's cotton farm in Mississippi. Wynette's father was a farmer and guitarist who died when Tammy was eight months old. She was raised by her grandparents while her mother worked in a defense plant in Birmingham, Alabama.

Wynette married her first husband just before finishing high school. When her marriage began to fall apart, she moved to Birmingham and became a licensed beautician. Troubled, Wynette allowed her thoughts to turn to song. She auditioned and won a regular spot on a Birmingham television show. She spent the better part of 1965 making frequent trips to Nashville hoping to gain a recording contract. She got serious about her ambition in January 1966, when she moved with her three kids to Nashville.

Wynette's first record was her cover of Bobby Austin's "Apartment Number 9," released in October 1966. The honky-tonkin' "Your Good Girl's Gonna Go Bad" followed in February 1967 and made it to the country Top Five. In July 1967 Wynette

Her days as a Birmingham beautician still in the recent past, Tammy Wynette seduces the camera during an early publicity session, circa 1966. Wynette's biggest hits, though often overproduced, are characterized by the singer's remarkably effective interpretation of emotional lyrics.

husband, restless heart George Jones. The king and queen of country music, they dueted on several hit records. After they were divorced in 1975, they continued to record together. Altogether, Wynette has been married five times (Wynette's current husband-manager, George Richey, was the organist at her fourth wedding).

Wynette was named Country Music Association Female Vocalist of the Year in 1968, 1969, and 1970, the first artist to have won three years in a row. She has recorded more than 50 albums, and her performing career extends into the 1990s. In 1992 she recorded the dance tune "Justified and Ancient" with the KLF, and it went on to become a worldwide hit.

did an about-face with a heart-tugging duet with David Houston, "My Elusive Dreams." With embellishment by producer Billy Sherrill's sea of chorus and strings, the recording became Wynette's first number one in a long line of hit records. Her follow-up hit, "I Don't Wanna Play House," earned her a Grammy in 1967.

Wynette hit her stride with the 1968 anthem "Stand By Your Man," which she cowrote with Sherrill. It won a second Grammy for her. She titled her 1979 autobiography *Stand By Your Man*.

But even as Wynette was enjoying the success of "Stand By Your Man," she married her third

At her peak in the seventies (above), Wynette scored an international hit in the nineties (below) with "Justified and Ancient," a collaboration with Scottish dance/rappers the KLF.

TAMMY WYNETTE

Real name: Virginia Wynette Pugh

Born: May 5, 1942; ItawaMba County, Mississippi

First hit: "Apartment Number 9" (1966)

Other notable hits: "Your Good Girl's Gonna Go Bad" (1967), "I Don't Wanna Play House" (1967), "My Elusive Dreams" (with David Houston, 1967), "D-I-V-O-R-C-E" (1968), "Stand By Your Man" (1968), "We Loved It Away" (with George Jones, 1974), "You and Me" (1976)

Awards and achievements: Grammy, Best Country and Western Solo Vocal Performance—Female (1967, 1969); Country Music Association (CMA) Female Vocalist of the Year (1968, 1969, 1970); Academy of Country Music Female Vocalist of the Year (1969)

THE STATLER BROTHERS

The Statler Brothers are known for smooth harmonies and songs that brim with bittersweet nostalgia. From left, they are Jimmy Fortune (who replaced original member Lew DeWitt in 1982), Phil Balsley, and brothers Harold and Don Reid. Their harmonies define the word "smooth."

Their biggest hits include their first and best-known song, "Flowers on the Wall," which resulted in a pair of 1965 Grammys. The Statlers continued their horticulture theme with 1970's "Bed of Rose's." They won their third Grammy in 1972 for "The Class of '57," a ballad about the realities of adulthood.

In recent years the Statlers have remained in the limelight by expanding outside of music. They played themselves in *Smokey and the Bandit II*, starring Burt Reynolds, and in 1991 they began hosting a regular variety show on The Nashville Network.

What do the Statler Brothers have over country legends Johnny Cash, Merle Haggard, and George Jones? They have more Country Music Association (CMA) awards.

The Statler Brothers are nine-time recipients of the CMA's Vocal Group of the Year award, including an unprecedented six-year string of victories between 1972 and 1977.

None of the quartet is actually named Statler, and just two are actually brothers. When they first hit the road in 1963 with Johnny Cash, the group was looking for a name. Harold Reid, bass vocalist, saw a box of Statler Tissue in the corner of a dressing room and chose the name. His brother, emcee Don Reid, has often pointed

The members of the quartet first sang together in Staunton, Virginia, in 1955. Original member Lew DeWitt is at the far right in this 1977 photo.

out, "We could have been known as the Kleenex Brothers."

The gospel-influenced vocal quartet hails from rural Virginia. Besides the Reid brothers, the original Statlers consisted of Philip Balsley, tenor, and Lew C. DeWitt, baritone. In 1982 Jimmy Fortune replaced DeWitt, who retired because of ill health.

THE STATLER BROTHERS

Real names: Don Reid; born June 5, 1945; Staunton, Virginia

Harold Reid; born August 21, 1939; Augusta County, Virginia

Philip Balsley; born August 8, 1939; August County, Virginia

Lew C. DeWitt; born March 8, 1938; August County, Virginia

First hit: "Flowers on the Wall" (1965)

Other notable hits: "Bed of Rose's" (1970), "The Class of '57" (1972), "I'll Go to My Grave Loving You" (1975), "How to Be a Country Star" (1979), "Charlotte's Web" (1980)

Awards and achievements: Grammy, Best New Country & Western Artist (1965); Grammy, Best Contemporary (R&R) Performance Group (Vocal or Instrumental) (1965); Grammy, Best Country Vocal Performance by a Duo or Group (1972); Country Music Association (CMA) Vocal Group of the Year (1972, 1973, 1974, 1975, 1976, 1977, 1979, 1980, 1984)

CHARLEY PRIDE

Charley Pride was a baseball player before he was a country singer. In the mid-1950s, the twilight years of baseball's Negro Leagues, he was a member of the Memphis Red Sox. After a two-year stint in the service, Pride joined a semipro team in Helena, Montana, in the summer of 1960. One night Pride sang between the games of a double header. The response was so strong that Pride got a part-time gig at a local country club.

Pride went on to become the first successful black singer in country music history, just as his hero Jackie Robinson was the first successful black player in major-league baseball history.

Pride was born on March 18, 1938, in Sledge, Mississippi. He was the only one of the ten children who was interested in music. He started listening to Hank Williams records, and by the time Pride was 14 he had saved enough money from working in the cotton fields to buy his first guitar, a Sears Silvertone.

For all his rugged rural roots, Pride's baritone has always been slick—due in great part to the smooth technique imparted by Nashville producer Jack Clement. Clement's understated approach shaped Pride's biggest hits—"Just Between You and Me," "Snakes Crawl at Night," his 1965 break-through single; 1971's "Kiss An Angel Good Morning"; and "Is Anybody Goin' to San Antone?"

Pride has settled in Dallas and returned to his original inspirations—sports and Hank Williams. Two of his 1980s recordings were a cover of Williams's "Honky Tonk Blues" and a rollicking tribute to the local football team, "Dallas Cowboys."

Kiss an angel good morning: Charley Pride is congratulated after being awarded a gold record for his album, The Best of Charley Pride.

CHARLEY PRIDE

Born: March 18, 1938; Sledge, Mississippi

First hit: "The Snakes Crawl at Night" (1965)

Other notable hits: "Just Between You and Me" (1966), "Is Anybody Goin' to San Antone?" (1970), "Kiss an Angel Good Morning" (1971), "You're My Jamaica" (1979), "Honky Tonk Blues" (1980)

Awards and achievements: Grand Ole Opry member (1967); Country Music Association (CMA) Entertainer of the Year (1971); CMA Male Vocalist of the Year (1971, 1972); Grammy, Best Sacred Performance (1971); Grammy, Best Gospel Performance (Other Than Soul Gospel) (1971); Grammy, Best Country Vocal Performance, Male (1972); five number-one country hits in a row (1969-1971); six gold records (1970 and 1972)

Deep in the timbre of a George Jones song, you can hear the soul of country music. The absolute purity of Jones's vocals assures that his style will never go out of fashion.

Jones is a Country Music Association male vocalist of the year representing a range of two decades—he won in 1962 and 1963, when the award was still voted on by country disc jockeys, and in 1980 and 1981. He sings from the most cobwebbed corners of his heart. His textured voice reveals tension, with authoritative range running like a railroad train between honky-tonk and sorrow.

Jones's trademark is his playful country flutter. He downcasts vocal lines for drama before immediately climbing the scale. This is what emphasizes tension in his 1986 classic, "Wine-colored Roses."

Jones was born on September 12, 1931, in rural Saratoga, Texas. "I never played guitar until church, although when I was very young, I sung around the house," Jones told the Chicago *Sun-Times* in a rare 1988 interview. "My Sunday school teacher taught me my first chords on a guitar. I would go with Sister Annie and Brother Berle Stevens into this little town called Kuntz, Texas. Every Saturday afternoon, we'd sit inside the car with loudspeakers on the outside. Sister Annie would play guitar and I'd sing harmony with her or she'd sing harmony with me."

His mother, Clara Jones, was very religious and played organ and piano in church. His father, George Washington Jones, was a hard-living truck driver and pipe fitter. On the side, he played a little "square dancin' guitar," as

Jones puts it. Clara was a Pentecostal who often shielded young George and his six brothers from the fallout of their father's drinking binges.

As a youngster, Jones listened to the Grand Ole Opry on KRIC in Beaumont, Texas. Hank Williams, Sr., came to town in 1949 to play live on KRIC. Williams sang "Wedding Bells" with Eddie and Pearl, the husband-and-wife house band that featured an excitable 19-year-old George Jones on electric guitar. Jones was so hyper about playing behind Williams that he never hit a note.

"Hank sat and talked with us like he knew us his whole life," Jones told the *Sun-Times*. "I worshipped him. His style was all in the feeling. He could sing anything and it would make you

sad, but an up-tempo thing could make you happy."

And Jones's early recordings were happy. In 1953, the year Jones was discharged from the U.S. Marines, he signed with the Houston-based Starday label, for whom he recorded hits such as "Why Baby Why" and "Uh Uh No." But what followed were raw rockabilly singles, such as "Rock It" and his own version of "Heartbreak Hotel" (recorded under the pseudonym Thumper Jones to avoid upsetting traditional country fans). In fact, Jones's first number one record, "White Lightning" (on Mercury Records), was written by rockabilly star J. P. "The Big Bopper" Richardson in 1959.

"I feel bad about it nowadays," Jones said in 1988. "I feel bad

Above: *During his formative flattop years, George Jones often played on buses and in high school gymnasiums in Texas.* Opposite: *The publicity photos had become slicker by the late 1960s, but the power of Jones's vocals had not been tamed.*

THE NEXT GENERATION: THE 1960s AND 1970s

York. Jones has been sober since 1986.

In March 1983 Nancy and George Jones left Nashville to open "Jones Country Music Park" near Beaumont. "It saved my life and everything else," Jones said in a 1991 biography for MCA Records. In 1988 Jones was ready to put his full effort back into recording and he sold the park and moved back to Nashville.

"You've done this for so many years, you just enjoy being out there in front of those people," he said in his record company biography. "As long as they like me, I'll do it 'til I die."

because I love country music so much. I tried to buy up all the old [Starday] masters so people couldn't hear them anymore. It was such a bad sound."

After several years with Mercury, Jones moved to United Artists Records and had Top 10 hits like 1962's "She Thinks I Still Care," 1963's "We Must Have Been Out of Our Minds" (a duet with Melba Montgomery), and a 1964 pop crossover with "The Race Is On." In the 1970s Jones sang with artists as diverse as Johnny Paycheck, James Taylor, Ray Charles, and of course his ex-wife, Tammy Wynette.

One can chronicle the turbulent Jones-Wynette marriage through the high-strung hit singles they had as a duet: 1972's "Take Me," 1973's "Let's Build a World Together," and 1980's "Two Story House." Jones and Wynette became the parents of a daughter,

Georgette. In 1975 Wynette divorced Jones after seven years of marriage.

Unfortunately, Jones acquired his father's taste for alcohol. After missing 54 concerts, he earned the nickname of "No-Show Jones." He filed for bankruptcy in 1979 and checked himself into a hospital. He attempted to dry out again in 1982, but in 1983 he was arrested in Mississippi for cocaine possession and public intoxication. The next day he flipped his car and nearly killed himself. His weight had dropped from 160 to 105 pounds. Texas singer-songwriter Ray Wylie Hubbard tried to sing some sense into Jones by writing the song, "George, Put Down That Drink."

The terminally shy Jones credits much of his survival to his fourth wife, Nancy Sepulveda Jones, whom he married in 1983. The Louisiana native met Jones in 1980 at a Jones concert in upstate New

---

GEORGE JONES

Born: September 12, 1931; Saratoga, Texas

First hit: "Why Baby Why" (1955)

Other notable hits: "White Lightning" (1959), "She Thinks I Still Care" (1962), "We Must Have Been Out of Our Minds" (with Melba Montgomery, 1963), "The Race Is On" (1964), "Take Me" (with Tammy Wynette, 1972), "Bartender's Blues" (1978), "He Stopped Loving Her Today" (1980)

Awards and achievements: Country Music Association (CMA) Male Vocalist of the Year (1962, 1963, 1980, 1981); Grammy, Best Country Vocal Performance, Male (1980); CMA Single of the Year (1980); CMA Music Video of the Year (1986)

COUNTRY MUSIC STARS

CONWAY TWITTY

Conway Twitty scored the biggest hit of his career, "It's Only Make Believe," in 1958. For some years after that, he was pegged as a rock 'n' roll heartthrob.

Conway Twitty has had 63 Top 10 hits on the *Billboard* country charts. He had a string of 30 straight number-one country hits going until 1977. Twitty has a handle on what he does, and he does it very well: He sings songs to women.

"You don't bite the hand that feeds you, and women buy most of the records," Twitty told Mike Boehm of the *Los Angeles Times* in a 1991 interview.

Twitty was born Harold Jenkins on September 1, 1933, in Friars Point, Mississippi. As a youngster Twitty was exposed to the primitive guitar sounds and raw harmonica of the rural blues movement. He has claimed that the blues affected his development more than listening to the Grand Ole Opry.

Twitty was five years old when he began playing guitar and picking up songs from his father, who was a ferryboat pilot on the Mississippi River. During his teens, Twitty's family moved to Helena, Arkansas. He formed the Phillips County

Ramblers, a country-blues band that landed a weekly gig on KFFA, the same radio station that broadcast *King Biscuit Time* with blues legend Sonny Boy Williamson.

Twitty also began to excel in baseball but was sidetracked from a career with the Philadelphia Phillies organization because of the draft. After being discharged from the army in 1956, he gravitated to the rockabilly sound coming out of Sun Studios in Memphis.

Sun owner Sam Phillips got Twitty in the studio, but Phillips was unhappy with the results. Nothing was released. Twitty rebounded by finding a manager who encouraged him to continue on the path of rock 'n' roll but suggested a snazzier stage name. Twitty turned to a map and found Conway, Arkansas, and Twitty, Texas.

In 1958 Twitty scored his biggest hit, "It's Only Make Believe," a dramatic ballad that echoed with the sexuality of a young Elvis Presley. The song soared to number one on the pop

In Loretta Lynn, Twitty found a congenial duet partner. Together, they notched hit after hit in the seventies.

charts. He continued to sing penitent pop ballads until 1965, when he crossed over to country. Twitty's successful duets with Loretta Lynn in the early 1970s gave him added credibility.

Twitty also became known in Nashville for shrewd business deals. In 1982 he opened the Twitty City tourist attraction in Nashville. In late 1991 he announced the development of "Twitty Bird," a line of wild bird feed.

Twitty still charms his audiences with a cunning country flutter in his restrained baritone. In 1985 he told the Associated Press how a Twitty hit is made: "A young couple is listening to the jukebox, the song comes on, he squeezes her hand at the right moment, they are happy, and Conway Twitty has a hit record."

CONWAY TWITTY
Real name: Harold Lloyd Jenkins
Born: September 1, 1933; Friars Point, Mississippi
First hit: "It's Only Make Believe" (1958)
Other notable hits: "Lonely Blue Boy" (1960) (rock), "Next In Line" (1968), "To See My Angel Cry" (1969), "Hello, Darlin'" (1970), "After the Fire Is Gone" (with Loretta Lynn, 1971), "She Needs Someone to Hold Her (When She Cries)" (1972)
Awards and achievements: Grammy, Best Country Vocal Performance by a Group (with Loretta Lynn, 1971); 22 Country Music Association (CMA) awards nominations; four CMA awards with Lynn; 30 consecutive number-one hits on the country charts until 1977; voted a "Living Legend" by readers of *Music City News* (1988)

Changing musical trends do not faze Twitty, who is unafraid to put his own spin on the hippest hits by others. In 1991 he began covering the Michael Bolton pop-metal tune, "Just the Thought of Losing You."

THE NEXT GENERATION: THE 1960s AND 1970s

The first shots from country music's outlaw movement can be heard in the early 1950s recordings of Lefty Frizzell, but in the '70s a restlessness invaded country music. On one side of Nashville, Waylon Jennings, Willie Nelson, and Kris Kristofferson were experimenting with a hybrid of country and rock. On the other side of town, producer Billy Sherrill's suburban string arrangements helped country cross over to pop.

Jennings dipped his toe in the outlaw pool as early as 1973 when he recorded *Honky Tonk Heroes*, an album of Billy Joe Shaver covers. Shaver was a spirited Texas songwriter whose iconoclastic

Above: Waylon Jennings, onetime bandmate of Buddy Holly, rocks out in the mid-'60s. Below: By 1985, Jennings was firmly established as one of country's best vocalists and most intriguing personalities.

themes were perfect for Jennings's deep and surly vocals.

"That album was a turning point for me," Jennings said in a 1991 interview with the Chicago *Sun-Times*. "And it was a turning point for music in Nashville in general. It was everything that music in Nashville wasn't at the time. Some of those songs didn't have but three instruments on them."

Jennings came into the world on June 15, 1937, in Littlefield, Texas. His father was a sharecropper and a truck driver who, on the side, played guitar and harmonica in a local band. But it was Jennings's mother who taught him his first guitar chords.

Jennings left school in the tenth

grade (he earned his General Educational Development certificate in 1990) and moved to Lubbock, Texas, to work as a deejay. He met Buddy Holly in 1955 and was quickly hired as a bass player in Holly's band.

Holly died on February 3, 1959, in a plane crash near Mason City, Iowa, along with J. P. "The Big Bopper" Richardson and Ritchie Valens. Jennings was supposed to have been on the plane too, but he had given up his seat on the plane to his boss, Richardson. His survival is part of rock 'n' roll legend.

Jennings regrouped, and spent the early sixties in Phoenix,

performing in clubs and recording for several labels. In 1965 he was signed to RCA Records by Chet Atkins who produced *Folk Country*, Jennings's awkwardly titled debut LP for the label.

In 1969 Jennings married his fourth and present wife, singer Jessi Colter. She figured in the historic 1976 compilation album *Wanted: The Outlaws*, which also featured Jennings, Willie Nelson, and Tompall Glaser. *Wanted: The Outlaws* was the first Nashville album to go platinum (selling 1,000,000 copies). It was the start of a new movement. Jennings went on to become a superstar of country music.

Top right: *Country music's "outlaw" movement received national exposure in April 1979, when Waylon Jennings appeared on NBC-TV's* Midnight Special.
Above: *Outlaw image aside, the fact remains that Jennings has sold a tremendous number of records, and earned a great deal of money for himself and for his label, RCA.*

WAYLON JENNINGS
Real name: Waylon Arnold Jennings
Born: June 15, 1937; Littlefield, Texas
First hit: "Stop the World (And Let Me Off)" (1965)
Other notable hits: "Only Daddy That'll Walk the Line" (1968), "The Taker" (1970), "Good Hearted Woman" (with Willie Nelson, 1976), "Are You Ready for the Country?" (1977), "Luckenbach, Texas" (with Willie Nelson, 1977), "I've Always Been Crazy" (1978), "Highwayman" (with Johnny Cash, Willie Nelson, and Kris Kristofferson, 1985), "If I Can Find A Clean Shirt" (with Willie Nelson, 1991)
Awards and achievements: Grammy, Best Country Performance by Duo or Group (with the Kimberleys, 1969); Grammy, Best Country Vocal Performance by Duo or Group (with Willie Nelson, 1978); Country Music Association (CMA) Male Vocalist of the Year (1975); CMA Single and Album and Vocal Duo of the Year (with Willie Nelson, 1976); 16 number-one singles; nine gold albums; two platinum albums; two double platinum albums; one quadruple platinum album

A deeply interpretive singer, Willie Nelson makes Nashville bend for him instead of letting Nashville force his distinctive music into traditional country.

Nelson was born on April 30, 1933, in Abbott, Texas. When he was very young, his parents divorced. He and his older sister, Bobbie, were raised by their grandparents.

Nelson's ears were tuned into all kinds of music. He heard late-night jazz from a New Orleans radio station and piano boogie-woogie from Freddie Slack. One of Nelson's earliest and lasting influences was Frank Sinatra.

In 1943, Nelson got his first professional job as an acoustic guitarist with the Bohemian Polka Band in nearby Fort Worth. By the time he reached high school, Nelson had joined The Texans, a loose country aggregation fronted by his brother-in-law.

After less than a year in the Air Force, Nelson obtained a medical discharge for a chronic back injury. He rejoined The Texans and in 1952 married Martha Mathews, a 16-year-old Cherokee Indian carhop. In pursuit of a career as a farmer, Nelson moved to Waco, Texas, and enrolled in Baylor University. To pay for his college education, Nelson sold vacuum cleaners and Bibles door to door.

After two years Nelson dropped out of college and became a disc jockey in San Antonio, which led to other radio gigs in California, Texas, and Vancouver, British Columbia. In the fall of 1956, while working at KVAN radio in Vancouver, Nelson decided to cut a record of his own. It was an

Above: *Many country music insiders are convinced that Willie Nelson—seen here in long-ago 1965—is the best songwriter Nashville has ever produced. By the mid-'70s he was a preeminent country performer, as well. Opposite: As Nelson's epic career rolled into the 1990s, he remained committed to touring, spending more than 200 days on the road every year.*

original composition, "No Place For Me," with a Leon Payne tune, "Lumberjack," on the flip side. Nelson pressed 500 copies of the single on his own and sold them over the radio at a dollar apiece. "No Place For Me" is regarded as Nelson's rarest recording.

Nelson returned to Texas in 1957 and eventually settled in Pasadena, where he continued to pursue songwriting while working as a disc jockey. During this time he wrote "Family Bible" and "Night Life." But Nelson felt he was going nowhere fast in Texas, and in 1960 he took off for Nashville in a beat-up 1946 Buick.

Nelson intended to be a songwriter, but after hanging around Tootsie's Orchid Lounge in downtown Nashville, he was hired in 1961 as a bass guitarist in Ray Price's band, the Cherokee Cowboys. Offstage, Nelson's songwriting began to blossom. In 1961 he wrote "Crazy" for Patsy Cline, "Funny How Time Slips Away" for Billy Walker, and "Hello Walls" for Faron Young. Nelson was signed by Liberty Records in 1962.

By 1964 Nelson had become a regular on the Grand Ole Opry. The rest of the '60s saw Nelson achieve moderate success as a performer, although he was becoming increasingly disenchanted with the lush strings and emotive backing choirs that were defining the Nashville Sound.

After a December 1970 fire gutted his house, Nelson returned to Texas. He divorced his second wife, Shirley Collie, with whom he had recorded, and in April 1971 he married his third wife, Connie. Nelson's commercial break-

Nelson and friend Waylon Jennings (right) celebrated the 59th birthday of the Grand Ole Opry on the 1984 television show The Door is Always Open.

Nelson said. "Fortunately, all those years of waiting, I had some songs that I'd written that I could live off of and that let me keep my band together and keep my show on the road. Or else I'da had to have folded long ago. Gone back to selling encyclopedias door-to-door."

But Nelson turned an about-face on the red-bandanna outlaw image in 1978 and released the resplendent album *Stardust*, a collection of pop standards. In recent years he has branched out into film—he had a major role in the 1979 film *The Electric Horseman*, and in 1980 he costarred with Dyan Cannon in *Honeysuckle Rose*. He has also devoted much of his free time to heading the Farm Aid movement, which raises money for American farmers.

In late 1990, the Internal Revenue Service seized Nelson's property to ensure payment of $16.7 million in back taxes. Two of Nelson's ranch homes and many personal items were auctioned off to raise money. He recorded a

through came in 1972 when he signed with Atlantic Records. In February 1973 he recorded three albums' worth of material while holed up for five days in a New York City studio. His band included his pianist sister Bobbie, Doug Sahm of the Sir Douglas Quintet, Larry Gatlin, and western swing fiddle player J. R. Chatwell.

In 1974 Atlantic dissolved its country division, and Nelson moved to Columbia, which gave him complete control over product. His debut album at Columbia was 1975's *Red-Headed Stranger*, and it was a smash. Nelson also had a Top 10 hit with "Blue Eyes Crying in the Rain."

Nelson followed up the success of *Red-Headed Stranger* with 1976's *Wanted: The Outlaws*, which combined Nelson with Waylon Jennings, Jessie Colter, and Tompall Glaser. Even though the album featured reissued material from Nelson's earlier years, it hit number one on the country charts

and crossed over into the Top 10 on the pop charts.

Nelson's "outlaw" image was forever imbedded in country music culture. In 1978 he told *Rolling Stone* writer Chet Flippo how he made Nashville work for him. "I waited 'til the time was right,"

Willie Nelson at the 1975 CMA awards show. At the same event a year later, Nelson launched country music's "outlaw" movement with a rave-up rendition of Lefty Frizzell's "If You've Got the Money, I've Got the Time."

mail-order album, *Who'll Buy My Memories,* to pay off the debt. It contains demos of 25 songs whose rights were seized by the IRS.

"There's nothing precious in life except loved ones," Nelson told the Associated Press in 1991. "All of these things I've lost are just things." Nelson's comment was an eerie prophecy. On Christmas Day, 1991, his only son, Billy, committed suicide at the age of 33.

But the show will remain on the road. Nelson's storied life has been about bending, but never breaking.

WILLIE NELSON

Real name: Willie Hugh Nelson

Born: April 30, 1933; Abbott, Texas

First hit: "Willingly" (with Shirley Collie, 1962)

Other notable hits: "Touch Me" (1962), "Blue Eyes Crying in the Rain" (1975), "If You've Got the Money, I've Got the Time" (1976), "Good Hearted Woman" (with Waylon Jennings, 1976), "My Heroes Have Always Been Cowboys" (1980), "On the Road Again" (1980), "Highwayman" (with Waylon Jennings, Johnny Cash, and Kris Kristofferson, 1985)

Awards and achievements: Grand Ole Opry member (1964); Grammy, Best Country Vocal Performance, Male (1975, 1978, 1982); Grammy, Best Country Vocal Performance by a Duo or Group (with Waylon Jennings, 1978); Grammy, Best Country Song (1980); eight Country Music Association awards; National Academy of Popular Music "Lifetime Achievement" (1983); ACM Pioneer Achievement Award (1992); seven gold albums; nine platinum albums; two triple platinum albums

Nelson has donated a considerable portion of his free time to the Farm Aid movement; between 1985 and 1992, he helped coordinate five Farm Aid benefit concerts that raised almost $20 million.

Mel Tillis has stuttered since he caught malaria as a three-year-old. He has since made the affliction work for him by using stuttering as comic relief during concert performances. An early 1980s album was called *M-M-Mel Live*. He even titled his 1985 autobiography *Stutterin' Boy*.

But Tillis's real gift has been the ability to articulate the blend of a country shuffle with classic pop melody. Among his 500 compositions are the Kenny Rogers and the First Edition hit "Ruby, Don't Take Your Love to Town" and "Detroit City," which was a Top 10 hit for Bobby Bare.

His "Ruby . . .," the story of an impotent Vietnam Vet begging his wife to stay with him, illustrates that Tillis doesn't shy away from challenging subject matter. Tillis's lesser-known "Commercial Affection" deals with prostitution. His 1968 hit, "Who's Julie," details the trauma of a wife hearing her husband talking in his sleep.

Tillis was born on August 8, 1932, and raised in Pahokee, Florida. He learned guitar as a child but didn't play professionally

Accomplished as both singer and songwriter, Mel Tillis has been an important figure in country music for more than 35 years.

At a 1988 concert in Southern California, Tillis wrapped his baritone around the ballad "You'll Come Back (You Always Do)," written by novelist Norman Mailer for the film Tough Guys Don't Dance.

until 1956, when he dropped out of the University of Florida. "I'm Tired," his first composition, was a number-one hit for Webb Pierce. Tillis went on to have regional success with "The Violet and the Rose" and "Finally," recorded for Columbia Records, his first label.

Although Tillis was defined as a songwriter during his early years in Nashville, his commercial break was a gruff baritone reading of the Harlan Howard classic "Life Turned Her That Way."

Tillis's most recent number-one hit was "Southern Rains," in February 1981. His daughter is country singer Pam Tillis, who enjoyed success on the country charts a decade later.

MEL TILLIS

Born: August 8, 1932; Pahokee, Florida

First hit: "The Violet and the Rose" (1958)

Other notable hits: "Wine" (1965), "These Lonely Hands of Mine" (1969), "Good Woman Blues" (1976), "Burning Memories" (1977), "I Believe in You" (1978), "Southern Rains" (1981)

Awards and achievements: Country Music Association (CMA) Entertainer of the Year (1976); coproduced and costarred in 20th Century–Fox film *Uphill All the Way* with Roy Clark (1985)

ROY CLARK

Even though Roy Clark was once best known as a banjo player, he will always be associated with the *Hee Haw* television series, which he co-hosted with Buck Owens between 1969 and 1986. Clark remained with the show in the 1990s. A generation of country music fans came to know Clark for his cornball humor and toothy smile.

What was forgotten was that Clark got his first recording contract in 1962 with Capitol Records after spending three years as a crack session player behind rockabilly star Wanda Jackson. Or that one of the highlights of Clark's recording career was *Makin' Music*, a swinging 1979 MCA album that paired Clark with Texas bluesman Clarence "Gatemouth" Brown.

Clark was born on April 15, 1933, in Meaherrin, Virginia. His first instrument was the banjo. Having won regional banjo competitions, Clark appeared on the stage of the Grand Ole Opry when he was eight years old.

After his first hit record, "Tips of My Fingers" in 1963, Clark drifted off into television. He never came back. Clark was already fast friends with country television star Jimmy Dean. After his hit records came out, he appeared on Johnny Carson's *Tonight Show* as well as the *Andy Williams Show*, the *Mitzi Gaynor Special*, and *Sammy and Company*. He even dropped in for a cameo on *The Odd Couple* comedy series.

Today Clark tours occasionally, performs at his own theater in Branson, Missouri, and earns a nice income from *Hee Haw* syndication.

A banjo whiz by the age of four, Roy Clark later became a top session guitarist. Today, he may be America's most visible "picker."

ROY CLARK
Born: April 15, 1933; Meaherrin, Virginia
First hit: "Tips of My Fingers" (1963)
Other notable hits: "Yesterday, When I Was Young" (1969), "Thank God and Greyhound" (1970), "Riders in the Sky" (1973), "The Lawrence Welk Hee Haw Counter Revolution Polka" (1973), "Honeymoon Feelin'" (1974), "If I Had to Do It All Over Again" (1976)
Awards and achievements: Academy of Country Music Top Country Comedy Act (1969); seven Country Music Association (CMA) awards including Entertainer of the Year (1973), Comedian of the Year (1970), and Instrumentalist of the Year (1977, 1978, 1980); Hollywood Boulevard Walk of Fame star (1975); Grammy, Best Country Instrumental Performance (1982)

To the detriment and benefit of his career, Roy Clark never met a television camera he didn't like; he's been active in the medium since the mid-'50s. His long tenure as co-host of television's Hee Haw has kept him in the public eye and paid him handsomely, but has also obscured his virtuosity as a musician.

onnie Milsap got into country music at an older age, which caused him to bring a bolder perspective to the traditional form. He was 29 when his first country album, *Where My Heart Is*, was released on RCA in 1973. At that time Milsap's heart was precisely into rhythm and blues. In the mid-1960s he had opened for such blues artists as Bobby "Blue" Bland. It's not surprising, then, that on *Where My Heart Is* Milsap sings such songs as Merle Haggard's "Branded Man" with soulful vocals backed by a gritty band. Milsap's voice has never bent toward the twangy intonations of traditional male country singers.

Milsap was born on January 16, 1944, in Robbinsville, North Carolina. He did not understand that he was blind until the age of five, when he was enrolled in the North Carolina State School for the Blind. At that school he learned to play violin, piano, and guitar—all before he was 12 years old.

Rock 'n' roll was Milsap's first love. As a teenager he formed a

Although he is best known as a country singer, Ronnie Milsap has also done session work that includes the piano backup on the Elvis Presley pop hits "Suspicious Minds" and "Kentucky Rain."

Milsap has flirted with pop music for much of his career. Regardless, he maintains a large country following, as witness this appearance on TV's Hot Country Nights.

rock band, the Apparitions, with three other blind musicians. After working as a sideman for country-rocker J. J. Cale, Milsap moved to Nashville in 1973, where he had immediate success.

He won a 1974 Grammy for best male country vocal performance for "Please Don't Tell Me How the Story Ends" and in 1976 repeated in the same category with "(I'm a) Stand By My Woman Man." By 1985, when he charted the Mike Reid–Troy Seals composition "Lost in the Fifties Tonight (In the Still of the Night)," Milsap was regarded as a pop star more than as a country singer.

RONNIE MILSAP

Born: January 16, 1944; Robbinsville, North Carolina
First hit: "I Hate You" (1973)
Other notable hits: "A Pure Love" (1974), "Please Don't Tell Me How the Story Ends" (1974), "(I'm A) Stand By My Woman Man" (1976), "Lost in the Fifties Tonight" (1985), "Don't You Ever Get Tired (of Hurting Me)" (1989)
Awards and achievements: Grammy Award, Best Male Country Performance (1974, 1976, 1985); Country Music Association Entertainer of the Year (1977)

SONNY JAMES

They called Sonny James the "Southern Gentleman," and he has done nothing to disturb that charming persona since he broke onto the country charts in 1953 with "That's Me Without You."

In the innocent late '50s and early '60s, James was country music's answer to Pat Boone. He is best known for ballads about unrequited love—"Young Love," which was his first legitimate pop hit in 1957, and 1965's emotional "Behind the Tear." And in 1973 James produced the Marie Osmond pop hit "Paper Roses."

James was born Jimmie Loden on May 1, 1929, in Hackleburg, Alabama. He was raised in a show business family—his first performance was at the age of four. The Loden Family won first place at a folk contest in Birmingham,

The lightly likeable sound of Sonny James propelled the singer to heavy chart success in the latter part of the 1960s.

Alabama. According to myth, singer Kate Smith was a judge. She bestowed a silver dollar on the littlest Loden, predicting great things ahead in show business.

James's career started to take off after he finished serving a two-year military stint in Korea in 1952. Chet Atkins befriended him and introduced him to a producer at Capitol Records, where he stayed until 1972, when he switched to Columbia.

James's impression of innocence survived the social change of the mid-'60s. He had 16 consecutive number-one country hits between 1967 and 1971. At the same time, his career took some strange twists. He appeared in the low-budget film *Las Vegas Hillbillys* with Jayne Mansfield. And his 1977 album, *In Prison, In Person*, was produced by Tammy Wynette's husband George Richey inside the Tennessee State Prison. It featured James backed by the Tennessee State Prison Band.

Although Sonny James was dismissed by some as country music's answer to Pat Boone, he did record his share of grittier material, including covers of Ivory Joe Hunter's "Since I Met You Baby" and Roy Orbison's "Only the Lonely."

SONNY JAMES

Real name: Jimmie Loden

Born: May 1, 1929; Hackleburg, Alabama

First hit: "That's Me Without You" (1953)

Other notable hits: "For Rent" (1956), "Young Love" (1957), "First Date, First Kiss, First Love" (1957), "The Minute You're Gone" (1963), "Baltimore" (1964), "A World of Our Own" (1968), "That's Why I Love You Like I Do" (1972), "When the Snow is on the Roses" (1972)

Awards and achievements: *Billboard's* number one country artist (1969), three Grammy nominations (1965), *Record World* magazine Record of the Year award (1965), 16 consecutive number-one country hits (1967-1971)

DOLLY PARTON

For many people Dolly Parton is country music. That is paradoxical, because by the 1990s Parton has changed from country vocalist to uplifting pop stylist. And if she isn't known for pop singing, then she is recognized through her film and television appearances. In 1991 film critic Roger Ebert asked, "Do people realize how good Dolly Parton is? Or do her popularity and her image get in the way? Parton's voice is genuinely original, not only strong and pure, but also filled with character and humor. She reads a lyric as well as anybody in popular music."

Parton comes from some of the most unpolished roots in contemporary country music. She was born January 19, 1946, in the impoverished mountain region of Locust Ridge, Sevier County, Tennessee. She was the fourth of a dozen children. Her father could not read or write.

The feisty Parton began singing as soon as she could talk. When she was eight, an uncle gave her a small Martin guitar, her first musical instrument. From that time on, Parton wanted to be a star.

Parton has never forgotten her poor roots. Some of her best-known songs reflect the early days of her life: "Tennessee Mountain Home," "Coat of Many Colors," and "Eagle When She Flies." Parton performed the last song in dramatic fashion before President George Bush at the 1991 Country Music Association (CMA) awards at the Grand Ole Opry.

"That song ['Eagle When She Flies'] is about an Appalachian mother with a kid on her hip and one in her belly and two hanging on her legs, stirrin' a pot of beans," Parton told Los Angeles writer Luaine Lee in 1991. Such humble material was perfect for Parton's small soprano. Her voice

knew when to glitter and when to glide, a feature that helped her pop crossover.

Parton was the first member of her family to graduate from high school. The day afterward she headed to Nashville. During her first day in town she met a shy asphalt-paving contractor named Carl Dean, whom she married in 1966. In an industry where marriage is a dicey proposition, the Parton-Dean marriage has survived.

Before her marriage, Parton was living with Bill Owens, an uncle who was a part-time songwriter. In 1966 Parton and Owens wrote "Put It Off Until Tomorrow," a Top 10 country hit for Bill Phillips (Parton can be heard singing harmony on the record). The success with Phillips led Parton into her own deal with Monument Records. Her loquacious debut, "Hello, I'm Dolly," was released in 1967. Among her first Monument hits was 1967's "Dumb Blonde," one of the few songs Parton has recorded that she didn't write or cowrite. She has published more than 3,000 songs.

Her combination of Smoky Mountain wit, blond wigs, an impressive bosom, and long false fingernails was beginning to attract real attention. Country star Porter Wagoner, looking for a singer to replace Norma Jean on his television and road show, turned to Parton.

THE NEXT GENERATION: THE 1960s AND 1970s

They were an immediate success. Mixing Wagoner's tenor harmony with Parton's lead melody produced such hit singles as 1968's "The Last Thing On My Mind" and 1969's "Always, Always." The CMA voted them vocal group of the year in 1968. But when time permitted, Parton still recorded on her own. Her 1970 ballad about a female mule skinner, "Mule Skinner Blues," became her first Top Five song. Her next release, "Joshua," reached number one.

Left: *Never shy about her fabulous figure, Parton has turned her shape into one of her most charming assets.* Above: *Dolly's warbling soprano brings unmatched feeling and sincerity to her recordings.*

Although Parton left the Wagoner show in 1974, he continued to produce her records for two more years. In 1976, looking to update her sound, Parton signed with Katz, Gallin and Cleary, a Los Angeles–based management company. Wagoner reacted bitterly and filed a lawsuit. Other Nashville figures also questioned Parton's move, but she maintained, "I'm not leaving country, I'm taking it with me."

And Parton took off. Her 1977 album, *Here You Come Again,* went platinum and won Parton her first Grammy. The follow-up album, *Heartbreaker,* went gold in 1978. Parton covered rock classics in 1979's *Great Balls of Fire,* which also went gold.

By the 1980s, a polished sound had evolved, but it wasn't because Parton's voice had lost its country charm. It was because Parton was surrounding herself with lush, upbeat pop arrangements and

contemporary rock musicians. For example, her middle-of-the-road "Islands in the Stream" duet with Kenny Rogers was one of only two singles in the entire music field to go platinum in 1983.

Parton and Rogers toured together in the late 1980s, although Parton suffered from health problems. Numerous concerts were cancelled due to a throat ailment. In 1987 her five-foot-two-inch frame dropped to 103 pounds.

In a 1977 article titled "What would you get if you crossed Mae West with Norman Vincent Peale?" *Rolling Stone* writer Chet Flippo confronted Parton with the story of a chesty stripper named Blaze Starr who used her natural attributes to escape poverty from the mountains of the mid-South. "Okay, I thought about being a stripper," Parton admitted. "But I decided that I really better not. I didn't want to get married. All I had ever known was housework and kids and workin' in the fields. But I didn't want to be domestic, I wanted to be free. I had my songs to sing, I had an ambition and it burned inside me. It was something I knew would take me out of the mountains. I knew I could see worlds beyond the Smoky Mountains."

In the fall of 1990, Parton received an honorary degree from Carson-Newman College in Jefferson City, Tennessee. She brought down the house at the commencement ceremonies when she called herself "Dr. D. D.," as a reference to her married name, Dolly Dean, as well as her bust size.

Some things you cannot get away from.

DOLLY PARTON

Born: January 19, 1946; Locust Ridge, Sevier County, Tennessee

First hit: "Dumb Blonde" (1967)

Other notable hits: "Mule Skinner Blues (Blue Yodel No. 8)" (1970), "Coat of Many Colors" (1971), "Jolene" (1974), "Is Forever Longer than Always?" (with Porter Wagoner, 1976), "Here You Come Again" (1977), "9 to 5" (1981), "Islands in the Stream" (with Kenny Rogers, 1983)

Awards and achievements: Grammy, Best Country Vocal Performance, Female (1978, 1981); Grammy, Best Country Song (1981); Grammy, Best Country Performance By a Duo or Group with Vocal (with Linda Ronstadt and Emmylou Harris, 1987); seven Country Music Association (CMA) awards (1968, 1970, 1971, 1975, 1976, 1978, 1988); Academy Award nomination (1980)

Monument Records tried briefly to push Parton as a pop singer in the mid-'60s, but eventually saw the light and let her follow her instincts. Over the years, she has written an amazing number of superior songs—some bouncy and infectious, others sober and contemplative. The very best draw on her own background as an impoverished mountain girl who longed for happiness and nice things. As versatile a singer as she is a songwriter, Parton makes any song uniquely her own.

Country music witnessed more dramatic change between 1980 and 1990 than in any previous decade. The 1980s were ushered in with the calculated glitter of the Urban Cowboy movement. The 1990s began more honestly, with the sincere promise of a new breed led by Garth Brooks, Mary-Chapin Carpenter, and Reba McEntire.

Country music has always prospered in times of economic recession, and America's fortunes were on the temporary downslide in both 1980 and 1990. But where the 1980 films *Urban Cowboy* and *Coal Miner's Daughter* (the latter based on the life of singer Loretta Lynn) were Hollywood concoctions that existed almost independently of country music, the roots of the new breed of star were firmly planted in the country-music tradition.

The Urban Cowboy fad died out because the songs that resulted from it were too calculated, and lacked lasting appeal. But Nashville nevertheless took its cue from Hollywood, at least for a while, and produced overly accessible records with emphasis on string sections and saccharine pop rhythms. It was in such an arena that Crystal Gayle, Kenny Rogers, Olivia Newton-John, and other slick pop-country artists flourished in the early eighties.

Musical conformity continued to define Nashville in the middle of the decade. Perky Barbara Mandrell popularized country-pop in Las Vegas, while Lee Greenwood—a former Vegas blackjack dealer—brought a Las Vegas persona to country. Longtime country fans were puzzled: Country music hardly seemed "country" at all, and lacked the passion that had characterized it in earlier years.

Above: The slickly packaged Mandrell Sisters, from left, Louise, Barbara, and Irlene. Below: Crystal Gayle, sister of Loretta Lynn, incorporated pop, light rock, and blues into her country repertoire. Far right: Sweet pop rhythms characterized the mock-country sound of Australian Olivia Newton-John.

But something interesting was bubbling beneath the glitzy surface: a "cowpunk" movement that opened the doors for younger acts that played country music in a rock 'n' roll landscape. Those musicians included Jason and the Nashville Scorchers, Steve Earle, Dwight Yoakam, and Marty Stuart.

Sparked by the cowpunkers in the late 1980s, Nashville record companies shifted progressive artists from country to pop divisions. That left fertile space for acts like Brooks, Clint Black, Alan Jackson, Vince Gill, Trisha Yearwood, Pam Tillis, and Kathy Mattea. These performers represent a new breed who were raised on a variety of musical influences—but who chose country.

The other significant reason for the rise of the new country artists is that they proved to be highly marketable—they excited listeners (even George Bush professed to be a country-music fan) and sold a lot of records. Even better, they led cosmopolitan yet squeaky-clean lives. Clint Black does not allow his entourage to drink before shows; Garth Brooks studied advertising in college; K. T. Oslin learned the showbiz ropes while a singer on Broadway. Country music has changed—just ask rowdy redneck Hank Williams, Jr., who was CMA entertainer of the year in 1987 and 1988, but who was not even nominated in 1991.

Above: *Country music reached a mass audience in the early 1990s via TV's* Hot Country Nights. *Among those present in the group seen here are Reba McEntire, Ricky Van Shelton, and Aaron Tippin. Far left: K. T. Oslin had had experience as a Broadway chorus girl and singer of commercial jingles before finding success with a pleasingly sophisticated sort of country music. Below: Positioned near the front of the pack of neo-traditionalists is honky-tonk disciple Dwight Yoakam.*

Thanks largely to this new direction, country music weathered the difficult recession of the early nineties better than any other form of popular music.

Mass-audience awareness of country music remained high, yet seemed to run deeper than in the early eighties. Television provided a further boost in 1990, when the Country Music Association (CMA) Awards ceremony became the top-rated show in its time slot. The success of the broadcast gave NBC-TV the impetus to schedule a regular Sunday night variety show called *Hot Country Nights,* which made its well-publicized debut in November 1991.

Even though country music prospered during the 1980s, it remained a difficult decade for women artists. Those who did enjoy success—Dolly Parton, Reba McEntire, Rosanne Cash, K. T. Oslin—crossed over into pop and rock. According to Robert K. Oermann, country-music writer for *The Nashville Tennessean,* women accounted for 38 percent of country chart action in the early 1980s but the figure had dropped to just 12 percent by 1990. One explanation may be industry leadership, for in 1991 only two major Nashville song publishing companies were headed by women.

The dilemma of female artists aside, it is clear that the country shuffle of the nineties has considerably more substance than it did during much of the eighties. Country's new breed seems intent upon shaping the future of the music while maintaining the integrity of its past. By any measure, it will be a pleasurable and fascinating evolution.

ALABAMA

The supergroup Alabama helped bring country music to young audiences in the 1980s. The group's great commercial success was due as much to its canny use of pop stylistics as to the solid musicianship of its members. From left, Alabama is Teddy Gentry, Jeff Cook, Randy Owen, and Mark Herndon.

Perhaps it's the captivating non-conformist outlaw image, but throughout the history of country music, rugged solo artists have over-shadowed most duets and groups. That is, until Alabama came along.

The band has been honored nine times by the Country Music Association (CMA), including being presented with the presti-gious Entertainer of the Year award in 1982, 1983, and 1984. Alabama has won a pair of Grammy Awards and from 1980 to 1987 notched 21 consecutive number-one records.

Alabama came together in Fort Payne, Alabama, a valley village of about 12,000 people at the foot of the Lookout Mountains. Socks, not music, had been Fort Payne's best-known product until Alabama rose to fame. Lead singer Randy Owen, keyboardist and lead guitarist Jeff Cook, and bass guitarist Teddy Gentry are cousins, but they didn't start playing together until 1970. Their first band was the ZZ Top-inspired Wild Country. Another cousin, Jackie Owen, was the group's first drummer. In 1979 he was replaced by Mark Herndon, a non-relative. Alabama's earliest

shows were at the Canyonland amusement park outside of Fort Payne.

In March 1973, Alabama left Fort Payne for Myrtle Beach, South Carolina. Thanks in part to the rapid turnover of the resort crowds, Alabama was able to perform an eclectic repertoire, including covers of rock hits by Bachman Turner Overdrive and Van Morrison, as well as rocking versions of country hits by George Jones and Merle Haggard.

By 1980 the group was leaning more heavily on original material, and had established its trademark acts like Garth Brooks and Clint Black, who utilized rock 'n' roll-style lighting, staging, and songs to cross over from country in search of a wider audience.

"We've not been innovators, but we've been close to what was happening," Randy Owen told the Associated Press in 1992. "We don't go for trends unless it makes the sound better. We've been able to adapt."

Alabama lead singer Randy Owen puts over a song at a June 1986 concert. After Alabama was given the Country Music Association's prestigious Entertainer of the Year Award in 1982, 1983, and 1984, the going got easier for other country groups, such as Exile and Shenandoah.

ALABAMA

Real names: Randy Owen; Jeff Cook; Teddy Gentry; Mark Herndon

Born: (Owen) December 13, 1949; Fort Payne, Alabama

(Cook) August 27, 1949; Fort Payne, Alabama

(Gentry) January 22, 1952; Fort Payne, Alabama

(Herndon) May 11, 1955; Springfield, Massachusetts

First hit: "My Home's in Alabama" (1980)

Other notable hits: "Tennessee River" (1980), "Old Flame" (1981), "Mountain Music" (1982), "The Closer You Get" (1983), "Southern Star" (1990)

Awards and achievements: Grammy Award, Best Country Performance by a Duo or Group with Vocal (1982, 1983); Country Music Association (CMA) Award, Entertainer of the Year (1982, 1983, 1984); CMA Award, Vocal Group of the Year (1981, 1982, 1983); CMA Award, Instrumental Group of the Year (1981, 1982); CMA Award, Album of the Year (1983); Academy of Country Music Artist of the Decade (1989); 21 consecutive number-one records 1980-1987

---

polished harmonies. Randy Owen's lead vocals, reminiscent of Glenn Frey of the Eagles, caught the ear of several record companies. That same year, Alabama signed with RCA Records.

Alabama sold 45 million records in the 1980s. By the time the 1990s rolled in, the group sounded more like a pop-rock band than a country band, especially in the acoustics of the big arenas in which they played. No longer as novel as they once were, Alabama has seen some of its rock-oriented appeal diminished by the advent of solo

Emmylou Harris began her musical career as a folk singer. In time, she established herself as a country-music traditionalist who drew from a wide variety of influences.

Contradiction has colored the life and career of Emmylou Harris. The daughter of a Marine Corps officer, she spent her formative years in music playing folk protest songs. She is a former straight A student and high school valedictorian who dropped out of the University of North Carolina. Professionally, she has propelled country music forward while embracing its past.

Harris was born on April 2, 1947 in Birmingham, Alabama. A "military brat" who moved frequently, she attended high school in Woodbridge, Virginia, where she was a cheerleader, a saxophone player in the school marching band, and winner of the "Miss Woodbridge" beauty pageant. Although she had an interest in folk music, she did not pursue music seriously until she went to the University of North Carolina and began singing at an off-campus pub called the Red Door. After dropping out of school, Harris

Below: *Harris formed her legendary Hot Band in 1975; that's Rodney Crowell on the far left. By 1990, though, Harris had abandoned the electric sound and returned to a purely acoustic style.*

headed for New York, where she sang at folk clubs in Greenwich Village.

Pregnancy and a failing marriage prevented Harris from following up on her first Jubilee Records album in 1969. Following her divorce, she stopped playing music and moved to Washington, D.C. to live with her parents. After a year of professional inactivity, Harris began playing country and folk clubs in the D.C. area. It was at the Cellar Door that she met the Flying Burrito Brothers, who introduced her to country-rock architect Gram Parsons. In Harris, Parsons found a female harmony singer; in Parsons, Harris found a mentor who broadened her horizons as a musician. The partnership was a fruitful one that ended tragically in 1973, when Parsons died at age 27 from a drug-induced heart attack shortly after he and Harris recorded "Grievous Angel."

Harris has since championed Parsons's progressive musical philosophy. She has recorded songs by writers as diverse as Merle Haggard, Bruce Springsteen, and Lennon & McCartney, and teamed up with Bob Dylan, Johnny Cash, and Bill Monroe. She shares one of her five Grammys with Linda Ronstadt and Dolly Parton, with whom she recorded the 1986 album, *Trio*. Alumni from her Hot Band include British rock guitarist Albert Lee, singer-songwriter Rodney Crowell, and bluegrass fiddle player Ricky Skaggs.

Harris's most recent affiliation is with the Nash Ramblers, an all-acoustic band featured on *Emmylou Harris and the Nash Ramblers at the Ryman*, a 1991 release recorded at Nashville's Ryman Auditorium, the home of the Grand Ole Opry for nearly three decades. Fittingly, then, Harris became the 70th member of the Opry in early 1992.

EMMYLOU HARRIS

Born: April 2, 1947; Birmingham, Alabama

First hit: "If I Could Only Win Your Love" (1975)

Other notable hits: "Sweet Dreams" (1976), "One of These Days" (1976), "(You Never Can Tell) C'est la Vie" (1976), "Mister Sandman" (1981), "If I Needed You" (with Don Williams, 1981)

Awards and achievements: Grammy Award, Best Country Vocal Performance, Female (1976, 1979, 1984); Grammy Award, Best Country Performance by a Duo or Group (1987); Country Music Association (CMA) Female Vocalist of the Year (1980); CMA Vocal Event of the Year (1988); Grand Ole Opry member (1992)

In 1970, when the Grand Ole Opry was still located in the Ryman Auditorium in downtown Nashville, Harris worked as a barmaid at the High Hat Lounge, just a few doors away. When she became a member of the Opry in 1992, Harris happily remarked, "It's like I've come home to a family I didn't even know I was part of."

THE JUDDS

Country values versus city values. That is how Naomi Judd once described the chemistry between herself and daughter Wynonna. Naomi was raised in rural Kentucky; Wynonna grew up in Los Angeles. Naomi likes the Stanley Brothers; Wynonna loves rocker Bonnie Raitt. Naomi's favorite color is white; Wynonna's is black.

But when they sang together, the Judds connected to make a musical rainbow. Loretta Lynn once said that harmony is the true soul of country music, and sure enough, it was Wynonna's saucy snarl that opened the doors for the Judds' exquisite harmonies, which were set in the blood-harmony tradition of the Louvin Brothers and the Delmore Brothers.

Naomi Ellen Judd was born January 11, 1946 in Ashland, Kentucky. Wynonna Ellen Judd was also born in Ashland, on May 30, 1964. The Judds first left their homeland in the mid-1960s, when they lived in various spots in the Midwest and the South.

In 1968 the family moved to Hollywood, California, where they lived until 1975. Naomi filed for divorce in 1972. While in Hollywood, she worked at different times as a secretary for the pop-soul group the Fifth Dimension and as a professional model. (That's Naomi on the sleeve of Conway Twitty's *Lost in the Feeling* record.)

In 1975 the Judds returned to Kentucky, settling in Morrill (population 50), where Naomi enrolled in nursing school.

"It was a conscious decision on my part," Naomi said in a 1987 record company biography. "I wanted my daughters to be close to our family, close to our heritage. And I wanted my children to learn where they come from and to have the freedom to develop their imaginations." Wynonna and her younger sister Ashley continued their educations.

Wynonna got her first guitar in 1976 and began singing with Naomi around the house. The more the Judds sang together, the more they enjoyed it. Soon they were mimicking the harmonies from every country duet album they could find in local used-record stores. The Judds returned to California in late 1976 and Naomi earned her nursing degree at a San Francisco hospital. While living in Marin County, Naomi bought a used 1957 Chevrolet, which was spotted by employees of Lucasfilm Company, who were shooting the sequel to *American Graffiti*. In rags-to-riches fashion, the film company rented Naomi's car, the Judds wound up becoming extras, and Naomi was hired as a secretary on the movie set. Naomi was bitten by the show-business bug more strongly than before. By May of 1979 the Judds had enough money to give Nashville a chance.

Once they settled in Nashville, the Judds experimented with their singing style by making homemade tapes on a K-Mart tape recorder. One such tape, featuring the Judds' harmonies accompanied by Wynonna on acoustic guitar, made its way to RCA Records in Nashville in 1983.

At their RCA audition, the Judds sang a 1936 bluegrass ballad, "The Sweetest Gift," which is about a mother who visits her son in prison. Ironically, the song was the first that the mother-daughter duo had learned together. RCA was impressed and the Judds were immediately signed to the label.

Following a December 1991 farewell concert, Naomi retired and Wynonna launched a solo career.

Within a year Naomi and Wynonna were jumping all over the country charts. Their first single, "Had a Dream," cracked country's Top 20. Their follow-up, "Mama He's Crazy," hit number one. The Judds went on to sell more than 10 million albums in an eight-year career. They consistently mixed sweet harmonies with Naomi's spunky show business initiative and flair for the dramatic.

"My daddy had a filling station, my mommy was a cook on a riverboat and we're from small-town America," Naomi told Kristine McKenna of the *Los Angeles Times* in 1987. "We never conceived in our wildest dreams that one day we'd be involved in the Technicolor adventure we're living today."

But every adventure must end. In 1990 Naomi was diagnosed with untreatable chronic hepatitis. On October 15, 1990 Naomi announced her retirement from performing—but only after a farewell tour that would last more than a year.

The Judds' final public performance was a pay-per-view cable special broadcast across the country on December 4, 1991 from Middle Tennessee State University.

"I have a fear of bridges," Naomi confessed to the *Chicago Sun-Times* a week before the concert. "I have had it all my life. Ashland [Kentucky] is on the Ohio River, and there is a big bridge there. I remember as a child, I'd hit the floor of the family car as we went over that bridge. So to me, the last concert is a bridge from

what has been the greatest eight years of my life into a total unknown."

The Judds were showered with accolades in their farewell year. They won two 1991 Grammys for the song "Love Can Build a Bridge" bringing their grand total to five Grammys—an impressive tally for an eight-year career. Nineteen ninety-one also brought the Judds their fourth consecutive

Country Music Association Award for Vocal Duo of the Year.

In February of 1992 Wynonna began her solo career with a bang: Her debut solo single, "She is His Only Need," debuted at number 30 on the 20-year-old *Radio & Records* country singles chart, making Wynonna the first female performer to manage the feat.

As her daughter toured as a solo artist, Naomi began work on her autobiography, which was projected to be turned into a four-hour miniseries for NBC-TV. She also assumed a greater role as a spokesperson for the American Liver Foundation.

Naomi (left) and Wynonna (right) are joined by Wynonna's sister, television actress Ashley Judd.

THE JUDDS
Real names: (Wynonna) Christina Ciminella; (Naomi) Diana Ellen Judd

Born: (Wynonna) May 30, 1964; Ashland, Kentucky
(Naomi) January 11, 1946; Ashland, Kentucky

First hit: "Had a Dream" (1983)

Other notable hits: "Mama He's Crazy" (1984), "Girls Night Out" (1985), "Rockin' with the Rhythm of the Rain" (1986), "Don't Be Cruel" (1987), "Born to Be Blue" (1990), "Love Can Build a Bridge" (1990)

Awards and achievements: Grammy, Best Country Performance by a Duo or Group with Vocal (1984, 1985, 1986, 1988, 1991); Country Music Association (CMA) Horizon Award (1984); CMA Vocal Group of the Year (1985, 1986, 1987); CMA Vocal Duo of the Year (1988, 1989, 1990, 1991); CMA Single of the Year (1985); 16 number-one singles; four gold, two platinum, and two double platinum albums

STEVE EARLE

Intense and troubled, Steve Earle signed a seven-album deal with MCA Records in 1986 but was without a label by 1992. His 1991 live album, Shut Up and Die Like an Aviator, *was a bizarre disaster.*

S teve Earle is the restless heart of modern country music. He made an imprint on Nashville with the 1986 album *Guitar Town*, which featured power-twang songs of the working class and drew critical comparisons to Bruce Springsteen and John Mellencamp. Since then, Earle has changed gears more often than a driver in the Indianapolis 500.

Earle was born January 17, 1956 in rural Texas. His father was an air-traffic controller who was often transferred around the San Antonio area. Earle ran away from home at age 14 to follow singer-songwriter Townes Van Zandt throughout the Lone Star State. Earle was on the road as a musician by age 16, married at 19, and in Nashville by 20, framing houses and digging swimming pools.

In 1981, after a second marriage which took place at the Take 5 Bar in Nashville's Metro Airport (he's been married three times since), Earle left Nashville for what he described as "two tequila-drenched years" in Mexico.

He returned to Nashville in 1983 when he signed with CBS. After one album of neo-rockabilly tunes, Earle left the label. In 1986 he moved to MCA, who gave him a seven-album deal. He followed up on the 1986 success of *Guitar Town* with 1987's *Exit 0*, which allowed a higher profile to the Dukes, Earle's roadhouse band.

In late 1988 Earle released *Copperhead Road*, a successful crossover album that incorporated the mandolin and other folk instruments, and featured traditional Irish rockers the Pogues. Conversely, 1990's *The Hard Way* was a dark album with metal overtones and songs that addressed abusive police and the death penalty. Earle sang "When the

Earle's working-class songs have been compared to songs by rock stars Bruce Springsteen and John Mellencamp. His song topics have included capital punishment and the auto industry.

Steve Earle has always considered himself an outsider. In the early 1990s he distanced himself from country music by producing the debut album of the Immigrants, a hard-rock group.

People Find Out" with backing vocals provided by the Christ Missionary Baptist Church choir of Memphis, Tennessee.

Earle has always been more than happy to confuse rock and country audiences. In the late 1980s he was an opening act for artists as diverse as the power-punk Replacements, country legend George Jones, and folk-rock icon Bob Dylan. He also played the Roxy and other Los Angeles rock clubs.

"There's a lot of technology now that can be used to make the message more powerful," Earle told the *Chicago Sun-Times*. "But the main point is the song, and great country music's main point is always the song."

Earle's 1991 release, *Shut Up and Die Like an Aviator,* was a distorted live album recorded during a tour where rumors of the singer's self-inflicted failing health abounded. His career ran aground and his fans were forced to await further developments.

STEVE EARLE
Born: January 17, 1956; near San Antonio, Texas
First hit: "Guitar Town" (1986)
Other notable hits: "Goodbye's All We Got Left" (1987), "Copperhead Road" (1989), "Nothing but a Child" (1989)
Awards and achievements: Number-one country album, *Guitar Town* (1986); top country artist in *Rolling Stone* magazine critics poll (1986)

LYLE LOVETT

Lyle Lovett is an imaginative singer-songwriter who has drawn praise from many of his peers. His fourth album, Joshua Judges Ruth, *explored not just country but jazz, gospel, blues, and swing.*

Lyle Lovett likes to toy with conventions. He's a fourth-generation Texan, but he's afraid of cows. He wears his hair tall, not short or long. He's touted as a country singer-songwriter, and while he does play shuffles and waltzes, he's just as likely to play honking blues or swinging jazz or somber folk music.

Although Lovett hasn't achieved broad radio airplay, his three albums on MCA have sold well thanks to positive reviews, widespread television exposure, and strong word-of-mouth among fans. His artistic standing was underlined when his album, *Lyle Lovett and His Large Band*, earned him a Grammy Award in 1989 for best country vocal performance by a male.

Lovett grew up in Klein, Texas, on the same plot of land where his great-great-grandfather, town namesake Adam Klein, first settled. Today, Lovett lives in a home once owned by his late grandfather, which is part of the ranch where his parents, William and Bernell Lovett, reside and raise cattle.

Lovett began singing and writing songs while earning degrees in journalism and German at Texas A&M. He met singer-songwriter Nanci Griffith by interviewing her for the school paper. With her support, he started playing small nightclubs in Houston, Dallas, and Austin.

While performing in a folk festival in Luxembourg in 1983, Lovett hooked up with the J. David Sloan Band and followed them back to Arizona. Backed by that band, Lovett recorded his first songs in a Scottsdale studio.

Lovett took his self-made tape to Nashville, where he received such encouragement that he returned to Arizona to record 14 more originals. Esteemed songwriter Guy Clark, a newfound Lovett fan,

One's eye goes immediately to Lovett's hair, and the singer will admit that it's become something of a gimmick. Regardless, Lovett's mile-high hairdo can't overshadow his talent and versatility.

passed the fellow Texan's new music to Tony Brown of MCA Records. Brown added a few instrumental parts to ten of Lovett's previously recorded songs and released them in 1986 as *Lyle Lovett*, which was critically acclaimed.

The first album revealed a singer-songwriter with a refined, assured vision and a witty way with words. His first disc also hinted at his ability to write swinging blues vamps with the song "An Acceptable Level of Ecstasy (the Wedding Song)." He expanded upon this talent in the *Pontiac* album, and then fully displayed his ability to blend jazz, blues, and country on his third album, *Lyle Lovett and His Large Band*, which featured his 11-piece, racially mixed touring band on several songs.

By the early 1990s, Lovett had contributed songs to several movie soundtracks. He also contributed a version of "Friend of the Devil" to a collection of Grateful Dead covers called *Deadicated*. His fourth album, *Joshua Judges Ruth*, was released in March 1992.

LYLE LOVETT

Born: November 1, 1957; Klein, Texas

First hit: "Farther Down the Line" (1986)

Other notable hits: "Cowboy Man" (1987), "God Will" (1987), "Give Back My Heart" (1987), "She's No Lady" (1988), "I Married Her Just Because She Looks Like You" (1989), "Here I Am" (1989)

Awards and achievements: Grammy Award, Best Country Vocal Performance, Male (1989)

Rodney Crowell began his career as a guitarist and writer in Emmylou Harris's legendary Hot Band in the 1970s. By 1988, he had established himself as a solo performer of unusual power.

Rodney Crowell represents the new wave of Nashville songwriters who have learned to minimize ornamentation. His carefully selected lyrics are a response to inner emotion instead of external rhetoric, and he admitted in a *Vogue* magazine interview to have been "as influenced by John Lennon and Bob Dylan as by Merle Haggard."

Crowell was born August 7, 1950 in Houston, which is where he grew up. He played drums in his father's honky-tonk band, learned hundreds of songs, and gained insights that would later help him as a songwriter and performer.

Crowell relocated to Nashville in 1972. He began to absorb the direct songwriting styles of other Texans living in the city, such as Guy Clark and Townes Van Zandt. Between 1975 and 1978 Crowell played acoustic guitar in Emmylou Harris's Hot Band, where he was pegged as the next Gram Parsons.

Harris recorded several Crowell compositions, including "Bluebird Wine" and "Ain't Living Long Like This."

In 1979 Crowell married Rosanne Cash, the daughter of Johnny Cash. They had three children before separating in early 1992. In 1987 Crowell produced Cash's *King's Record Shop,* which yielded four number-one country singles.

Although Crowell songs had become hit recordings by artists such as Bob Seger ("Shame on the Moon"), Crystal Gayle ("'Til I Gain Control Again"), and Jimmy Buffett ("Stars on the Water"), Crowell's breakthrough as a performer didn't come until 1988's *Diamonds and Dirt,* the fifth album of his career. The LP sparkled with five number-one country singles, all written, performed, and produced by Crowell—a first in country-music history. His stardom had become indisputable, and he seemed poised for even greater success. "After All This Time," a ballad from *Diamonds and Dirt,* was honored with a 1989 Grammy for Best Country Song.

RODNEY CROWELL

Born: August 7, 1950; Houston, Texas

First hit: "Stars on the Water" (1981)

Other notable hits: "I Couldn't Leave You If I Tried" (1988), "After All This Time" (1989), "Crazy Baby" (1989), "Many a Long and Lonesome Highway" (1990)

Awards and achievements: Grammy, Best Country Song (1989)

THE TEXAS TORNADOS

Only a state as big as Texas could conjure something as bawdy as the Texas Tornados. Members Freddie Fender, Doug Sahm, Augie Meyers, and Flaco Jimenez offer an irresistibly eclectic mixture of country music, conjunto (the accordion offering lead melody against a polka backbeat), and rhythm and blues.

Freddie Fender grew up in the Rio Grande Valley border town of San Benito. He is the best-known singer in the band, having scored with such hits as 1959's "Wasted Days and Wasted Nights" (re-recorded and sent to number one in 1975), the 1974 ballad "Before the Next Teardrop Falls," and the lilting 1976 hit, "You'll Lose a Good Thing."

Fender worked with vocalist Doug Sahm as early as 1959 at a sock hop in Sahm's hometown of San Antonio and again in the 1970s. The name "Texas Tornados" is derived from a nickname once bestowed on Sahm, a veteran of the 1960s rock band, Sir Douglas Quintet.

Blues-inspired organist Augie Meyers learned his minimalist four-beat style from bluesman Jimmy Reed, and contributed to "Mendocino" and other hits by the Sir Douglas Quintet. And Flaco Jimenez's conjunto accordion playing is practically legendary.

The Tornados first got together in late 1989 at Slim's, a San Francisco nightclub owned by rock singer Boz Scaggs. Warner Bros. was attracted to the idea of a Tex-Mex version of the Traveling Wilburys, and signed the Tornados.

"Soy De San Luis," a track from the group's self-titled debut album, won a 1990 Grammy for best Mexican-American performance. A follow-up recording, "Zone Of Our Own," received a 1991 Grammy nomination for Best Country Performance by a Duo or Group with Vocal.

Although Freddie Fender, seen here in 1979, had played with future Texas Tornados bandmate Doug Sahm as early as 1959, he wasn't sure the supergroup concept would work. After signing with Warner Bros. Records in 1990, Fender changed his tune.

THE TEXAS TORNADOS

Real names: Baldemar Huerta (Freddie Fender); Augie Meyers; Flaco Jimenez; Doug Sahm

Born: (Fender) June 4, 1937; San Benito, Texas
(Meyers) May 31, 1941; San Antonio, Texas
(Jimenez) March 11, 1939; San Antonio, Texas
(Sahm) November 6, 1942; San Antonio, Texas

First hit: "Hey Baby, Que Pasa" (1990)

Other notable hits: "Who Were You Thinkin' Of?" (1990), "Is Anybody Goin' to San Antone?" (1991)

Awards and achievements: Grammy, Best Mexican-American performance (1990); Grammy nomination, Best Country Performance by a Duo or Group with Vocal (1991)

The musical styles of the Tornados can stretch as far as the conjunto accordion of Flaco Jimenez (far left). The rest of the group, from left, is comprised of keyboardist Augie Meyers, onetime rocker Doug Sahm, and vocalist Freddie Fender.

GARTH BROOKS

Garth Brooks has set a new standard for country music success. In an unprecedented feat for a country artist, Garth's third album, *Ropin' the Wind,* reached the number-one spot on *Billboard*'s pop music charts the first week of its release. Only two previous country performers have ever reached the top spot on the pop charts—Johnny Cash in 1969 and Kenny Rogers in 1980, and they did so only after weeks of steady sales. Brooks's album, which was released in September 1991, started out at the top.

To the pop music industry, this brash country singer seemed to emerge from nowhere to capture the fancy of the American public. A native Oklahoman, Brooks was the sixth and last child to join the clan of Troyal and Colleen Brooks. The singer retains strong family ties to this day: his half-sister Betsy Smittle plays bass in his band, Stillwater. His brother Kelly travels with him as a tour accountant.

Though born into a musical family (his mother recorded for Capitol Records and appeared on the *Ozark Jubilee* in the 1950s), Brooks didn't pick up a guitar until he was a junior in high school. After graduation, he attended Oklahoma State University on an athletic scholarship as a javelin thrower.

While in college, Brooks started performing in nightclubs. At first he performed solo, offering his interpretation of songs by such personal heroes as James Taylor and Dan Fogelberg. Before long, he joined a band, mixing tunes by George Strait and Merle Haggard with those of the Georgia Satellites, Billy Joel, Bob Seger, and other rock bands.

Following a discouraging 1985 trip to Nashville, Brooks returned two years later, this time accompanied by his bride of one year, Sandy Mahl. Within days of his arrival, he was introduced to Bob Doyle, an executive at ASCAP (the American Society of Composers, Authors, and Publishers, which is a performing rights agency). Doyle's faith in Brooks's talent led him to leave ASCAP and form his own music publishing company, Major Bob Music, with Garth as his first client. Just eight months after Garth arrived in Nashville, he signed a recording contract with Capitol Records.

When Capitol introduced him to Allen Reynolds, a record producer who had also worked with Kathy Mattea, Don Williams, and Crystal Gayle, Garth's approach to music began to take shape. Reynolds produced Brooks's 1989 debut album, *Garth Brooks,* and would later produce *No Fences* and *Ropin' the Wind.* It was Reynolds who suggested that Brooks stop singing ballads in the full-voiced, operatic style associated with Gary Morris or Lee Greenwood. The producer encouraged Brooks to relax and sing in a gentler, more natural manner. Reynolds's coaching later proved to be a key to Brooks's success in conveying the tender emotion of the ballads "If Tomorrow Never Comes" and "The Dance." Both songs have since become signature hits for the young entertainer.

Garth's debut album also included the hits "Not Counting You" and "Much Too Young (To Feel This Damn Old)," the latter about a rodeo cowboy, a recurring subject in Brooks's songs. Of the four hits from the first album, Brooks wrote or cowrote all but "The Dance." He has since continued to write about half of the songs on his albums.

THE NEW BREED: THE 1980s AND 1990s

year for "The Dance" and the coveted Horizon Award, given to the artist who achieved the greatest career strides during the previous 12 months.

Since then, Brooks has become country music's biggest seller as well as a major award winner. The *No Fences* collection remained the number-one country album until the fall of 1991, when it slipped to number two as *Ropin' the Wind* took the top spot. By the start of 1992, his debut album had sold more than four million, while both *No Fences* and *Ropin' the Wind* topped the six million mark. The leading music industry trade magazines, *Billboard* and *Radio & Records*, selected Brooks as male country artist of the year. He

Brooks exudes an all-American appeal that is enhanced by his wife, Sandy, a onetime barrel racer in rodeo competition.

Garth Brooks sold 500,000 copies in its first year. Garth received the news of that milestone on May 24, 1990, the fourth anniversary of his marriage. By then, "The Dance" was a major hit, and the album sold another half-million copies in the month of June.

The sales of Brooks's albums have proliferated ever since. His second album, *No Fences,* sold 700,000 copies the first ten days it was in stores, thanks to the

blockbuster hit "Friends in Low Places." The first week of October 1990, both the first and second album crossed the million mark in sales. That same week, Brooks reached two more milestones: He became the 65th member of the Grand Ole Opry, and he was the most-nominated artist at the 1990 Country Music Association Awards.

Of his five nominations, Brooks won the award for video of the

---

GARTH BROOKS

Real name: Troyal Garth Brooks

Born: February 7, 1962; Tulsa, Oklahoma

First hit: "Much Too Young (To Feel This Damn Old)" (1989)

Other notable hits: "If Tomorrow Never Comes" (1989), "The Dance" (1990), "Friends in Low Places" (1990), "Unanswered Prayers" (1990), "The Thunder Rolls" (1991), "Shameless" (1991), "What's She Doing Now" (1992)

Awards and achievements: Grand Ole Opry member (1990); Country Music Association (CMA) Horizon Award (1990); CMA Entertainer of the Year (1991): CMA Album of the Year (1991); CMA Single of the Year (1991); Academy of Country Music Entertainer of the Year (1991, 1992); *Billboard* Male Country Artist of the Year (1991); Grammy Award, Best Country Vocal Performance (1991)

Whether Brooks can sustain his remarkable popularity remains to be seen, but for the moment he rides high on a canny blend of youthful and traditional appeal.

walked away with six Academy of Country Music awards in April 1991 and four Country Music Association awards the following October, claiming the prestigious Entertainer of the Year honors at both pageants. In 1992, he won American Music awards for best male country artist, best country single for "The Thunder Rolls," and best country album for *No Fences.* And at the '92 Grammy Awards, *Ropin' the Wind* picked up an award for best country vocal performance.

A lively, fiercely energetic concert performer, Brooks promises to keep taking chances and coming up with surprises. He also plans to be around awhile. "A big word for me is seven letters, something George Jones and George Strait have been able to do—sustain," he said backstage after being named Entertainer of the Year by the CMA. "I want to be here a long time and not be a flash in the pan."

A versatile singer, Travis Tritt handles country anthems and emotional ballads with equal skill. Although mindful of country-music tradition, Tritt has chosen not to link himself with Clint Black and other "new traditionalists."

Travis Tritt burst on the country music scene in late 1989 with his first single, "Country Club," and provided a new anthem for the working-class man. He also provided female fans with long-haired sex appeal.

Born February 9, 1963, in Marietta, Georgia, to James and Gwen Tritt, the singer grew up on his family's 40-acre farm.

He developed a love of music as a young boy and taught himself to play the guitar when he was only eight years old. By the time he was 14, he was writing songs. But his parents and his first wife, whom he married just three months after graduating from high school, discouraged his musical ambitions.

The marriage lasted less than two years, but Tritt's love of music continued. He pursued his ambi-

tion while working at a heating and air conditioning firm, but he exhausted himself with a heavy nighttime schedule of club dates.

By 1984, Tritt had left his day job and was making a meager living as a club act across Georgia. He married again, this time to Jodi Barnett, a woman who believed in his dream. Unfortunately, her intense involvement in his career overshadowed their relationship, and they divorced in 1989.

Tritt's professional breakthrough came in 1984, when he met Danny Davenport, a local pop promotion man for Warner Bros. Records. Davenport offered guidance and allowed Tritt to use his home recording studio. Over the next two years, they worked together and recorded enough songs for an album. Warner Bros. finally offered Tritt a record deal in 1988.

Tritt's debut album, *Country Club*, showcased his versatility with such diverse songs as the boisterous Southern rock tune "Put Some Drive in Your Country," the unabashedly country song "Drift Off to Dream," and the heartrending ballad "Help Me Hold On." The album went platinum in 1991, and Tritt won the CMA Horizon Award that same year.

It's All About to Change, Tritt's second album, contained more of the singer's eclectic brand of country music. Not part of the neo-traditionalists who dominated country music in the early 1990s (he avoids cowboy hats), Tritt has been more influenced by Hank Williams, Jr., than Hank Williams. "Here's a Quarter (Call Someone Who Cares)" and "Anymore" propelled the album to platinum status. Tritt's popularity was acknowledged by the music industry when he received two Grammy nominations (best male country vocal performance and best country song for "Here's a Quarter") in January 1992.

Tritt and "hillbilly rocker" Marty Stuart—who met and became friends at the summer 1991 Fan Fair—recorded a successful duet, "The Whiskey Ain't Workin'," in 1991 and embarked on a successful "No Hats" tour at the end of the year.

Like a lot of country stars, Tritt experienced hard going early in his career; even his family initially disapproved of his career choice.

TRAVIS TRITT

Real name: James Travis Tritt

Born: February 9, 1963; Marietta, Georgia

First hit: "Country Club" (1989)

Other notable hits: "Put Some Drive in Your Country" (1990), "I'm Gonna Be Somebody" (1990), "Help Me Hold On" (1990), "Here's a Quarter (Call Someone Who Cares)" (1991), "Anymore" (1991), "The Whiskey Ain't Workin'" (with Marty Stuart, 1992)

Awards and achievements: Grand Ole Opry member (1992); Country Music Association (CMA) Horizon Award (1991)

Vince Gill's haunting tenor voice has contributed to his considerable appeal. He is also regarded as one of the better guitar players in Nashville.

The only child of an Oklahoma City appellate judge, Vince Gill credits his father, who played banjo and guitar, for piquing his interest in music. An aspiring musician from an early age, Gill joined a local bluegrass band, Mountain Smoke, while still in high school.

Throughout the late 1970s and early '80s, Gill paid his dues with a number of diverse bands: Louisville-based Bluegrass Alliance; Boone Creek (with Ricky Skaggs); Byron Berline's Sundance; Pure Prairie League; and Rodney Crowell's Cherry Bombs. Through his friendship with the other Cherry Bombs, Gill landed a solo deal with RCA. Shortly after moving to Nashville in 1984, he recorded his six-song mini-album, *Turn Me Loose*. The success of the title track and "Victim of Life's Circumstances" brought him his first taste of national acclaim as a solo artist. He took home his first award when the Academy of Country Music voted him top new male vocalist.

Gill's second album, *The Things That Matter*, yielded two Top 10 hits, "If It Weren't for Him" (a duet with Rosanne Cash) and "Oklahoma Borderline." He then garnered more critical acclaim for *The Way Back Home*, his final album for RCA.

A move to MCA brought Gill the freedom to utilize the full range of his talent on *When I Call Your Name*. The album contains tunes ranging from dance hall swing to contemporary pop to rodeo songs. The first single, "Never Alone", which Gill wrote with Rosanne Cash, hit the Top 20. "Oklahoma Swing" was the

Gill became a member of the Grand Ole Opry in 1991. Here, he shares a moment with longtime Opry mainstay Roy Acuff.

strong follow-up hit from the album.

Another single, "When I Call Your Name," was Gill's first number-one hit and a Grammy winner in 1990. The following year, "When I Call Your Name" was elected best country song at the Grammy Awards.

Having proved his versatility with a wide range of songs on *When I Call Your Name,* Gill settled into a more clearly defined country style for his next album, *Pocket Full of Gold,* which was certified gold just five months after its release. The title tune, "Look at Us," and "Liza Jane" became instant hits.

Still reaping awards from his wave of success, Gill was a big winner at the 25th Annual Country Music Association Awards. He shared song of the year honors with Tim DuBois for "When I Call Your Name" and was also named male vocalist of the year.

Gill became a member of the Grand Ole Opry in 1991. The following year, he picked up a Grammy for "Restless," his vocal collaboration with Mark O'Connor, Steve Wariner, and Ricky Skaggs. A skilled golfer, Gill lives next to a Nashville golf course with his wife, Janis (cofounder of Sweethearts of the Rodeo), and daughter, Jennifer.

VINCE GILL

Born: April 12, 1957; Norman, Oklahoma

First hit: "Victim of Life's Circumstances" (1984)

Other notable hits: "When I Call Your Name" (1990), "Oklahoma Swing" (with Reba McEntire, 1990), "Never Alone" (1990), "Look at Us" (1991), "Pocket Full of Gold" (1991), "Liza Jane" (1991), "Take Your Memory With You" (1992)

Awards and achievements: Grand Ole Opry member (1991); Country Music Association (CMA) Song of the Year, Male Vocalist, Vocal Event (1991)

When George Strait first visited Nashville, he was told his music was behind the times. Looking back, it's clear he was a sign of the times, a bellwether who pointed the way to greater popularity and prosperity for country music.

At the beginning of the 1980s, the prevailing attitude among those running the country music industry was that Strait's blend of western swing, traditional honky tonk, and romantic ballads was old-fashioned and out of style. By the end of the decade, however, Nashville was singing a different tune, and Strait now stands tallest among the handful of artists who changed the sound and the look of country music.

In the decade following the release of *Strait Country*, the Texan's 1981 debut album, he racked up 25 number-one songs, five platinum albums for sales of more than one million, and 11 gold albums for sales of more than a half-million. His concert sales have topped $10 million annually since the late 1980s. He has twice received country music's most prestigious annual honor, the Country Music Association's entertainer of the year award. And he is cited as a primary influence by nearly every successful Nashville newcomer.

Strait was born May 18, 1952, the second of three children. His father was a junior-high math teacher and part-time rancher in Pearsall, Texas, a tiny settlement in the South Texas brush country located about 60 miles south of San Antonio. In his youth, Strait learned to ride horses and rope steers. His initial musical experience was singing "Louie, Louie" and other rudimentary rock songs with a garage band made up of high-school buddies. Shortly after graduation, he eloped to Mexico with his high-school sweetheart. Now, more than 20 years later, he and wife Norma still reside in South Texas with their son, George, Jr., born in 1981.

Strait joined the Army in 1971 and taught himself to play guitar a year later. In time, Strait's duties during his last year in the service consisted of performing country music on military bases.

Upon returning home, he enrolled in Southwest Texas State University in San Marcos. On campus, he pinned a note to a bulletin board advertising himself as a singer in search of a country band. He got a call from a group calling themselves Ace in the Hole. With Strait as lead singer, the band began performing nightly in honky-tonks within a 200-mile radius of San Marcos.

In 1979, Strait received a bachelor's degree in agriculture and started managing the family ranch, which by that time had grown to include more than 1,000 head of cattle. Despite the hard work of running the ranch, Strait continued to sing at night. The band's popularity grew, and Strait's voice became more confident and flexible with his nightly performances of traditional Texas dance hall music, which included healthy doses of songs made famous by Bob Wills, Hank Thompson, Johnny Bush, Lefty Frizzell, Merle Haggard, and George Jones.

In the late 1970s, Strait recorded a few songs for D Records, a Houston-based company owned by Pappy Dailey, who had given George Jones his first break more than two decades earlier. Strait's first single, "Ace in the Hole,"

THE NEW BREED: THE 1980s AND 1990s

received enough attention to give him the courage to travel to Nashville. He made the trek three times without getting a response.

In 1979, Strait figured he had given his dream a shot, and it was time to be more practical. He applied for several jobs, nearly accepting a position with a firm in Uvalde, Texas, designing cattle facilities. But Norma persuaded him to give music one more year.

Among his other supporters was Erv Woolsey, a former music industry executive who managed a San Marcos nightclub, the Prairie Rose, where the Ace in the Hole band often performed. In 1979, after Woolsey had returned to the music business as a promotion executive for MCA Records, he helped Strait arrange a Nashville recording session with producer Blake Mevis. The songs recorded during that session earned Strait a recording contract with MCA Records less than six months after he had turned down the job in Uvalde.

The first hit from Strait's debut album, *Strait Country*, was a stripped-down, dynamic Texas two-step titled "Unwound." It became the singer's first Top 10 hit, confounding those who thought radio wouldn't accept such a raw, traditional country style.

Strait has endured for more than a decade and has set several standards. In 1987, the Texan's *Ocean Front Property* disc became the first in country music history to debut at number one on *Billboard*'s country album chart. In 1990, Strait's hit, "Love Without End, Amen," became the first song since 1977 to remain in the number-one position on the country charts for five consecutive

Above: *Since Strait embraced traditional country attire in 1981, many other singers have followed suit.* Opposite: *Strait's polished brass rodeo-style belt buckle is a clue that the singer grew up on a ranch, and owns one today in South Texas.*

weeks. His 1991 hit, "Famous Last Words of a Fool," was the next song to repeat that feat.

Amid the success, he's also faced tragedy. His daughter, Jennifer, was killed at age 13 in an auto accident in 1986. At that point, Strait withdrew from interviews for more than a year, and now only reluctantly agrees to appear on television or talk to the press.

As for his music, Strait says: "I can't really see it changing very much. It's not that I set out to create a certain style or to change country music. It's just that I record the songs I like, and I do them in a way that feels right to me. It's worked pretty well so far, so I guess I'll keep doing it that way."

GEORGE STRAIT

Born: May 18, 1952; Pearsall, Texas

First hit: "Unwound" (1981)

Other notable hits: "Amarillo by Morning" (1983), "You Look So Good in Love" (1984), "Right or Wrong" (1984), "Does Fort Worth Ever Cross Your Mind?" (1985), "The Chair" (1985), "Ocean Front Property" (1987), "All My Ex's Live In Texas" (1987), "Love Without End, Amen" (1990), "Chill of an Early Fall" (1992)

Awards and achievements: Academy of Country Music (ACM) Top Male Vocalist (1984, 1985, 1988); Country Music Association Male Vocalist (1986); ACM Entertainer (1989)

THE NEW BREED: THE 1980s AND 1990s

RICKY VAN SHELTON

icky Van Shelton worked up his first song, a slow rocker called "My Conscience Is Bothering Me," on the guitar when he was 13. Absorbed at that time with rock, he discovered country music about a year later.

Shelton always believed he could make a living with his music. He honed his skills by performing as often as possible, and though this limited his social life, he did find time to meet his future wife, Bettye. The two were married in 1980.

With the support of his wife, Shelton moved to Nashville, where his homemade demo tape came to the attention of Jerry Thompson, a columnist for Nashville's morning paper, *The Tennessean.* Thompson alerted CBS Records executive Rick Blackburn, who agreed to watch Shelton perform in 1986.

Blackburn was impressed, and Shelton's professional career took off quickly. His first album, *Wild Eyed Dream,* yielded a Top 10 single, "Crime of Passion," and a number-one follow-up, "Somebody Lied." He was invited to appear on the Grand Ole Opry in June 1987 and was so enthusiastically applauded that he was called back for an encore — a rare occurrence on the Opry stage.

Wild Eyed Dream went platinum, and it brought Shelton a slew of awards in 1988. He was named top new male vocalist by the Academy of Country Music, the *Music City News* star of tomorrow, and the Country Music Association's Horizon Award winner. He also became a member of the Grand Ole Opry that year.

Shelton's second album, *Loving Proof,* went gold in eight weeks and later achieved platinum status.

Album number three, *RVS III,* continued the same mix of the old and the new, the honky-tonk music and the rockabilly that characterized Shelton's other work. With *RVS III,* the singer also enjoyed a similar rate of success, producing four Top Five hits — "Statue of a Fool" (a number-one remake of the Jack Greene classic), "I've Cried My Last Tear for You," "I Meant Every Word He Said," and "Life's Little Ups & Downs." Like his two previous albums, this best-seller was certified platinum.

Shelton followed up with *Backroads* in 1991, another collection of tunes demonstrating his rich, powerful country voice. Aside from indicating that Shelton was equally at home with a rocking backbeat or a soaring ballad, *Backroads* ventured into new territory with Shelton's duet with country superstar Dolly Parton. "Rockin' Years" became a chart-topper, which was accompanied by a music video eventually named CMT's number-one video of 1991.

RICKY VAN SHELTON

Born: January 12, 1952; Danville, Virginia

First hit: "Wild Eyed Dream" (1987)

Other notable hits: "Life Turned Her That Way" (1988), "I'll Leave This World Loving You" (1988), "Living Proof" (1990), "Statue of a Fool" (1990), "Keep It Between the Lines" (1991), "I Am a Simple Man" (1991), "Rockin' Years" (with Dolly Parton, 1991)

Awards and achievements: Grand Ole Opry member (1988); four platinum albums; Academy of Country Music top New Male Vocalist (1987); Country Music Association (CMA) Horizon Award (1988); CMA Male Vocalist (1989); TNN/*Music City News* Male Artist (1989, 1990, 1991)

KATHY MATTEA

Left and opposite: Some performers grow more cautious and calculated with their music as they become famous. Kathy Mattea has done the opposite: The more recognition she obtains, the more personal and innovative her music becomes.

L ike many country stars, Kathy Mattea spent several frustrating years in which she received little recognition. Her initial seven singles from her first two albums failed to crack the Top 20. Her career started to waltz forward in 1986 with her first Top 10 hit, the striking "Love at the Five and Dime." The follow-up, "Walk the Way the Wind Blows," also gusted into the Top 10, as did "You're the Power" and "Train of Memories." Then came "Goin' Gone" and "Eighteen Wheels and a Dozen Roses," both number-one songs.

The youngest of three children, Mattea was born June 21, 1959, in South Charleston, West Virginia. Her father worked at a Monsanto chemical plant; her mother was a housewife.

She attended school in nearby Nitro, took piano and tap dancing lessons as a child, and later learned to play the recorder and acoustic guitar.

In 1976, Mattea enrolled as an engineering student at West Virginia University in Morgantown. She hooked up with a folk group, Pennsboro, trading lead and harmony vocals with other members. Three years later, the group's lead songwriter, Mickey Pope, announced he was moving to Nashville to chase the big time. Mattea decided to go as well, leaving college despite her parents' objections.

Mattea teamed with Pope as a duet, appearing at songwriter nights until her partner decided to return to West Virginia a year after their arrival. Mattea remained, taking a job at the Country Music Hall of Fame as a tour guide. Later, she became a demo singer and began to perform at the Bluebird Cafe and other popular nightspots. These experiences led to a contract with PolyGram Records.

With the help of producer Allen Reynolds, Mattea overcame the sexy image dreamed up by PolyGram; with each successive album, her music grew more sparse and acoustic, her songs more earthy, her image more casual and softly feminine. In the end, the husky, fluid warmth of her vocal tone was allowed to come to the fore.

Mattea was named the female vocalist of the year by the Country Music Association in 1989 and 1990, and she won a Grammy Award in 1990 for her vocal performance on "Where've You Been," a song cowritten by husband Jon Vezner and Don Henry. The song also has won a CMA Award and Grammy Award for the writers. A solid performer, with much experience and talent behind her, Mattea should enjoy a lengthy career in country music.

KATHY MATTEA

Born: June 21, 1959; South Charleston, West Virginia

First hit: "Street Talk" (1983)

Other notable hits: "Eighteen Wheels and a Dozen Roses" (1988), "Goin' Gone" (1988), "She Came From Fort Worth" (1989), "Where've You Been?" (1990), "Asking Us to Dance" (1991), "Time Passes By" (1991)

Awards and achievements: Country Music Association (CMA) Single Record (1988); CMA Female Vocalist (1989, 1990); Academy of Country Music (ACM) Song of the Year (1988, 1989); ACM Top Female Vocalist (1990); Grammy Award, Best Country Performance Female (1990)

THE NEW BREED: THE 1980s AND 1990s

One of the new breed of performers to shake up Nashville in the 1980s, Reba McEntire became the reigning queen of country music by focusing on a traditional sound, recording consistently high-quality material, and remaining true to her roots. Along with George Strait and Ricky Skaggs, McEntire helped prove to Nashville that the strength and future of country music lay in its heritage. With more than 21 albums to her credit (including nine gold albums and three platinum), she continues to be one of country music's most popular entertainers.

McEntire was born in Chockie, Oklahoma, in 1955, the daughter of Jacqueline and Clark McEntire. Because her father was a champion steer roper, Reba, brother Pake, and sisters Susie and Alice grew up traveling the rodeo circuit with their parents. By the time she was in high school, McEntire competed in rodeo competitions as a first-class barrel racer and also sang as part of the Singing McEntires, the vocal group she formed with Pake and Susie.

Reba entered Southeastern Oklahoma State University in Durant, Oklahoma, in 1974, where she majored in elementary education. Despite her intentions to finish her education and become a teacher, McEntire was encouraged by her father to pursue a musical career. Singer Red Steagall, impressed by Reba's performance of the national anthem at the National Finals Rodeo, helped her land a recording contract.

McEntire debuted on Mercury/PolyGram Records in 1977 with the album *Reba*

Blessed with a voice that is as versatile as it is powerful, Reba McEntire is now the most popular female vocalist in country music.

McEntire. Newly married to Charlie Battles, she saw her records slowly enter the charts. "Three Sheets to the Wind," a duet with Jacky Ward (of "A Lover's Question" fame), reached the Top 20 in July 1978. Her second album, *Out of a Dream*, spawned the successful singles "Sweet Dreams," "Runaway Heart," and another duet with Ward, "That Makes Two of Us." The determined singer finally hit the Top 10 in 1980 with "(You Lift Me) Up to Heaven" and "I Can See Forever in Your Eyes," both from her *Feel the Fire* album.

The following year, country fans were hearing more hit songs from the lady with the powerhouse voice, including "I Don't Think Love Ought to Be That Way" and "Today All Over Again." She delivered another Top 10 hit, "I'm Not That Lonely Yet," the first

single from her fifth album, *Unlimited*.

McEntire's success soon snowballed, and by January 1983 she had her first number-one hit, "Can't Even Get the Blues." She followed up with "You're the First Time I've Thought About Leaving," which also went to number one.

Despite the success she was having with Mercury/PolyGram, McEntire's association with that label ended after the release of the ironically titled "There Ain't No Future in This." She went to MCA Records, where her soulful, emotional vocal style emerged in full force with her first MCA album, *Just a Little Love*. With "Every Second Someone Breaks a Heart," a song that edged closer to rock 'n' roll than she had ever gone before, McEntire made a conscious move to hold the attention of her younger fans and to build a larger following.

Momentum was rolling in McEntire's favor in 1984, when she was named the Country Music Association's female vocalist of the year; she went on to take the award each of the next three years — an unprecedented feat.

In 1985, McEntire had enough clout to begin coproducing her albums, starting with *Have I Got a Deal for You*. Her 1986 album, *Whoever's in New England*, began a new phase of accolades and acclaim. In October of that year, she was rewarded with CMA's

Opposite: McEntire has demonstrated a shrewd head for business by establishing her own management, publicity, and music-publishing companies. She remains very much in control of her career.

THE NEW BREED: THE 1980s AND 1990s

Opposite: *Born and raised in Oklahoma, McEntire once devoted much of her energy to rodeo competition. Happily for fans of country music, she forsook barrel racing for vocalizing.* Above: *Reba jams with (from left) Asleep at the Wheel's Ray Benson, Ricky Van Shelton, Colin Raye, and Aaron Tippin. Today, McEntire is in perpetual demand.*

a grinding plane crash en route to a concert. At the urging of Blackstock, she had skipped the flight, staying behind in San Diego to shake off a persistent case of bronchitis.

McEntire chose the songs for her next album, *For My Broken Heart*, to help her deal with the sorrow she suffered following the accident. She channeled all of her sorrows into making the album a universal statement on heartbreak and sadness, and her fans responded overwhelmingly. *For My Broken Heart* was certified platinum (signifying sales of more than one million copies) just two months after it was released in October 1991. McEntire reflected, "For me, singing sad songs often has a way of healing a situation. It gets the hurt out in the open — into the light, out of the darkness. I hope this album heals all our broken hearts."

coveted entertainer of the year award. In addition, her recording of "Whoever's in New England" garnered her a Grammy Award for best female country vocal performance.

Other awards included being named the Academy of Country Music's top female vocalist from 1984 through 1987; she was honored as the *Music City News* female artist of the year from 1985 through 1989; and she won the American Music Award for favorite female country vocalist from 1987 through 1989.

McEntire's career flourished, but her marriage to Charlie Battles suffered. In 1987, after 11 years of marriage, she left their 250-acre cattle ranch near Stringtown, Oklahoma, moved to Nashville, and filed for divorce. In early June of

1989, McEntire surprised her fans with an unexpected wedding to manager Narvel Blackstock. Originally a steel-guitar player in McEntire's band, the divorced father of three formed a management company with McEntire shortly after she left her former manager, Bill Carter, in 1987. In February of 1990, McEntire and Blackstock became the parents of a son, Shelby.

Not content to dominate country music, McEntire has dabbled in acting, beginning with her music videos and extending to a feature film (*Tremors*) and a TV miniseries (*Luck of the Draw: Gambler IV*).

Sadly, her good fortune was matched by terrible tragedy in 1991 when her road manager and seven members of her band were killed in

---

REBA McENTIRE

Born: March 28, 1955; Chockie, Oklahoma

First hit: "(You Lift Me) Up to Heaven," 1980

Other notable hits: "How Blue" (1985), "Whoever's In New England" (1986), "I Know How He Feels" (1988), "Cathy's Clown" (1989), "Fancy" (1990), "Rumor Has It" (1991)

Awards and achievements: Grand Ole Opry member (1985); Academy of Country Music Female Vocalist (1984, 1985, 1986, 1987, 1992); Country Music Association (CMA), Female Vocalist (1984, 1985, 1986, 1987); CMA Entertainer of the Year (1986); Grammy Award, Best Country Performance, Female (1986)

Dwight Yoakam's music is a celebration of traditional Americana. He scored his first hit with a revved-up version of "Honky Tonk Man," a song written in the mid-1950s by Johnny Horton. Yoakam loves Cadillacs and classic cars, and titled his first album Guitars, Cadillacs, Etc., Etc.

Dwight Yoakam roared his way into Nashville with his first album, *Guitars, Cadillacs, Etc., Etc.,* which was initially released on Oak Records and funded by $5,000 raised by the singer and his guitarist-producer, Pete Anderson. Reprise Records scooped up the rights to the recordings, asked Yoakam to add a few more songs, and distributed it nationwide. The first song, a kicking remake of Johnny Horton's "Honky Tonk Man," established Yoakam as a new musical force. For all of his success, though, Yoakam has been a vocal critic of Nashville.

He was born on October 23, 1956, in Pikeville, Kentucky, an impoverished small town in Pike Floyd Hollow, just a hike from Butcher Holler, the birthplace of Loretta Lynn. While Yoakam was still an infant, his parents, David and Ruth Ann, moved 90 miles north to Columbus, Ohio, where Dwight later became well acquainted with ridicule for his "hillbilly" accent.

Yoakam wrote his first song at age eight. By 1976, a year out of high school, he was performing throughout the Ohio Valley. Two years later, he arrived in Nashville, ready to dedicate himself to the style of music he loved. But Nashville found him "too country," so rather than compromise he moved to Los Angeles, where he drove an airport freight van by day while singing in working-class suburban honky-tonks at night.

Yoakam's roots-based brand of country caught on in L.A. and garnered him press coverage that provided the impetus for a return to Nashville. With the help of

Keenly interested in traditional country music, Yoakam has developed friendships with several country music legends, including Buck Owens (above, right), whom Yoakam coaxed out of retirement in the late '80s.

producer Pete Anderson, an educated young man dedicated to the raw, traditional forms of American music, Yoakam's vision became more defined, his attitude more uncompromising. The singer found favor fast, and his first two albums on Reprise Records sold 1.5 million copies in two years.

One of Yoakam's inspirations is Buck Owens, whom the young singer helped bring out of retirement. As Owens has related it, Yoakam simply showed up at Owens's Bakersfield office unannounced one afternoon. Yoakam then invited his idol to perform with him that night at a fair. Owens agreed, launching a comeback that would include a number-one duet with Yoakam ("Streets of Bakersfield") and two albums for Capitol Records.

Yoakam seems a mass of contradictions: He paved the way for country's new sounds by returning to its traditions; he criticized the Nashville industry while celebrating its performers; he has become hip by embracing the past. In doing so, he helped revitalize country music.

DWIGHT YOAKAM

Born: October 23, 1956; Pikeville, Kentucky

First hit: "Honky Tonk Man" (1986)

Other notable hits: "Guitars, Cadillacs" (1986), "Little Sister" (1987), "Streets of Bakersfield" (1988), "Turn It On, Turn It Up, Turn Me Loose" (1990), "You're The One" (1991)

Awards and achievements: Academy of Country Music, Top New Male Vocalist (1986); *Music City News* Vocal Collaboration (1989)

KENTUCKY HEADHUNTERS

With their debut album, *Pickin' on Nashville*, the Kentucky HeadHunters kicked open a door of new possibilities for country music. The quintet's initial collection of good-time, rockin' country blues has sold more than a million copies and attracted throngs of young, rowdy concert crowds who respond to the group's unorthodox stage antics and eclectic song selection.

The group's debut album garnered the group many major awards: They were named 1990 group of the year and producers of the year, and the record was selected as album of the year by the Country Music Association; they received a Grammy Award for best country performance by a group; the Academy of Country Music named them best new group of the year; *Billboard* magazine named them best group and best new artist; and the American Music Awards honored them as best new artist.

The huge level of success surprised everyone, including the close-knit band, which consists of two sets of brothers (singer Ricky Lee Phelps and bassist Doug Phelps; guitarist Richard Young and drummer Fred Young) and a cousin (guitarist Greg Martin). They hail from Arkansas and Kentucky and have varied backgrounds in rock 'n' roll, Southern boogie, and country.

The band signed with PolyGram, had fair success with the single "Walk Softly," and cracked the country Top 10 with "Dumas Walker." Two more hit singles — a cover of Don Gibson's "Oh, Lonesome Me" and "Rock 'n' Roll Angel" — and a high-profile tour as opening act for Hank Williams, Jr., kept the momentum going. The band's second album, *Electric Barnyard*, featured a rollicking, hilarious cover of "The Ballad of Davy Crockett," a remake of Bill Monroe's "Body and Soul," and a tribute to a live radio show in Kentucky they once hosted, *It's Chitlin' Time*. This album sold a million copies with little support from radio.

The rambunctious Kentucky HeadHunters (back row, from left): bassist Doug Phelps, singer Ricky Lee Phelps, guitarist Richard Young; (foreground, from left): drummer Fred Young, guitarist Greg Martin.

KENTUCKY HEADHUNTERS

Real names: Ricky Lee Phelps; Doug Phelps; Richard Young; Fred Young; Greg Martin

Born: (R. Phelps) October 8, 1953; Cardwell, Missouri

(D. Phelps) December 15, 1960; Paragould, Arizona

(R. Young) January 27, 1959; Metcalfe County, Kentucky

(F. Young) July 5, 1958; Metcalfe County, Kentucky

(Martin) March 31, 1953; Louisville, Kentucky

First hit: "Walk Softly On This Heart Of Mine" (1989)

Other notable hits: "Dumas Walker" (1990); "Oh, Lonesome Me" (1990), "Rock 'n' Roll Angel" (1990)

Awards and achievements: Country Music Association Group of the Year (1990, 1991); Grammy Award, Best Country Performance, Group with Vocal (1990)

The HeadHunters doing what they do best: performing live. A typical concert might include songs from sources as diverse as Hank Williams, Led Zeppelin, and blues legend Robert Johnson.

HAL KETCHUM

Hal Ketchum spent nearly 20 years building a reputation as a top-quality carpenter, and he approached a career in music with the deliberate patience of a master craftsman. When he was 38, his insistence on planning and quality paid off: "Small Town Saturday Night," his debut single, was one of the biggest country radio hits of 1991.

Singing about a small town seemed natural to Ketchum. He grew up in Greenwich, New York, a tiny town in the Adirondack Mountains near the Vermont border. His father, a foreman in a newspaper plant, was a banjo player and a member of the Buck Owens Fan Club. His grandfather was a concert violinist who also played square dances and led a swing band.

At age 15, Ketchum joined a rhythm-and-blues trio as a drum-mer. At the same age, he became a carpenter's apprentice, and by the 1980s he was an accomplished woodworker and furniture maker. He moved to Gruene, Texas, in 1981, where he did carpentry work, immersed himself in the region's rich folk-country music scene, and began to write songs and perform.

In 1986, he recorded his first album, *Threadbare Alibis*, for a small, independent European record company, Line Records. The folk-influenced literacy of his songs and understated warmth of his voice attracted attention in Nashville.

Ketchum signed first with Forerunner Music and later went with Curb Records. His critically acclaimed *Past the Point of Rescue* album featured "Small Town Saturday Night" and Ketchum's second hit, "I Know Where Love Lives."

Ketchum has two children from a previous marriage. In September 1991 he married Terrell Tye, president of Forerunner Music.

> **HAL KETCHUM**
> **Born:** April 9, 1953; Greenwich, New York
> **First hit:** "Small Town Saturday Night" (1991)
> **Other notable hits:** "I Know Where Love Lives" (1991), "Past the Point of Rescue" (1992)
> **Awards and achievements:** *Radio & Records* top country song of 1991

Before "Small Town Saturday Night," his country-music breakthrough, Hal Ketchum had been performing music and writing songs for 20 years. He calls his blend of folk and rock "American music." Ketchum's wife is Forerunner Music head Terrell Tye.

TRISHA YEARWOOD

In the late 1980s, when Garth Brooks and Trisha Yearwood made their livings as Nashville demo singers, Brooks promised Yearwood that if he got a break in the recording industry, he would do everything he could to help her. She pledged a similar pact with him. By 1991, Garth Brooks was a star, and when he learned that Yearwood had signed with MCA Records, he set her up with his management team and invited her to accompany him on tour as his opening act.

Yearwood's first hit, "She's in Love with the Boy," didn't need much assistance. A catchy story of young love, the hit pushed its way into the history books by becoming the first debut single by a female artist in 26 years to reach number one on the country music charts.

Her album, *Trisha Yearwood,* was released in July 1991 and sold more than 500,000 copies within three months. The album included two songs cowritten by Brooks,

Above and below: *Trisha Yearwood diligently worked her way up the country-music ladder, starting as an intern at a record company and ending up a star.*

"Like We Never Made a Broken Heart" and "Victim of the Game."

Trisha Yearwood grew up in Monticello, Georgia, a village of about 2,000 people some 60 miles from Atlanta. As a youngster she loved records by Elvis Presley and particularly Linda Ronstadt. Yearwood's first performance experience came in high school.

While a student at the University of Georgia, Yearwood realized that her heart belonged to music. With her parents' support, she transferred to Nashville's Belmont University and enrolled in its music business curriculum. While working toward her degree, she took a position as an intern in the publicity department at MTM Records. After graduation, she went back to work as a receptionist at the firm. Besides sharpening her understanding of the music industry, the work brought her in contact with many of the industry's

key players, as well as with her future husband, Chris Latham, an employee at EMI Music.

Despite being warned about a supposed industry and public bias toward female country music performers, Yearwood made a point to choose songs that represented a strong woman's point of view, passing over songs about "weak women" who forgive too easily. "That's What I Like About You," a song originally written for a male singer, is typical of Yearwood's forceful musical choices.

Concert audiences applaud Yearwood's expressive voice (she received an enthusiastic ovation after a power failure at one appearance forced her to sing her encore number, "When Goodbye Was a Word," a cappella). But success and constant travel brought problems, too, and Yearwood and Latham split up in 1991.

TRISHA YEARWOOD

Born: September 19, 1964; Monticello, Georgia

First hit: "She's in Love with the Boy" (1991)

Other notable hits: "Like We Never Made a Broken Heart" (1991), "That's What I Like About You" (1992)

Awards and achievements: Academy of Country Music New Female Vocalist (1992); her debut single was the first debut single by a female artist to go to number one on *Radio & Records* country chart (1992)

Opposite: *Whether in the studio or in concert, Yearwood enjoys offering her listeners the unexpected. From the start of her career, she has favored songs about strong women who make their own choices—good or bad.*

Left and opposite: *Alan Jackson has a legion of female fans, but the singer has more to offer than sex appeal. He's dedicated himself to a traditional style of country music. Indeed, Jackson has made no secret of his intense admiration for the legendary George Jones.*

Tall and handsome and dedicated to a traditional sort of country music, Alan Jackson has cultivated a legion of female fans who don't even mind that he's been happily married since 1980. In fact, it was his wife, Denise, who was largely responsible for his musical career.

In 1985, after a series of jobs that included driving a forklift at K-Mart and waiting tables at a barbecue restaurant, Jackson decided it was time to make the move from Newnan, Georgia, to Nashville. He wanted to try his hand at a career in music, though he had no idea where to go or who to see.

Denise, who had just quit teaching to become a flight attendant, saw singer Glen Campbell waiting for his luggage at the Atlanta airport and introduced herself. Explaining that her husband was about to move to Music City to pursue a career, she asked Campbell his advice. He gave her the name of his publishing company in Nashville and told her to have Alan drop by once they got

to town. Armed with Campbell's business card and a suitcase full of original songs, Jackson, with Denise at his side, relocated to Nashville.

He landed a job at The Nashville Network's mail room and began playing gigs at local hotels during the evenings. He put in countless hours polishing his songwriting skills and eventually landed a writing deal with Campbell's publishing company. With a $100-a-week draw as a staff songwriter, he was able to quit the mail room job and put his own band together. Booked by Campbell's organization, Jackson and the band played honky-tonks all across the country, five sets a night, five nights a week. Despite the hectic touring schedule and popularity he enjoyed on the club circuit, Jackson failed to stir any interest with the record companies.

A new manager, a young Australian named Barry Coburn, guided Jackson to Arista Records. Arista had just opened a country division in Nashville headed by Tim DuBois, former manager and

producer of Restless Heart. DuBois was looking for a great talent to launch Arista in Nashville, and he found that talent in Alan Jackson, who was signed to the Arista label in September 1989.

One month later, Jackson's debut single, "Blue Blooded Woman," reached radio stations nationwide. Arista followed up with the title cut from Jackson's debut album, *Here in the Real World*. On April 6, 1990, the Georgia native celebrated his first number-one record. The ensuing singles "Wanted," "Chasin' That Neon Rainbow," and "I'd Love You All Over Again" also hit number one, which spurred sales for *Here in the Real World*. The album soared to the number-four spot on *Billboard*'s country album chart and stayed in the Top 10 for over a year. It was certified gold in September 1990 and gained platinum status just six months later.

The Academy of Country Music named Jackson top new male artist in April 1991. Five days later, he shared song of the year honors with Mark Irwin for "Here in the Real World" at the Music City News Country Songwriters' Awards. "Wanted," which Jackson also penned, was another of the 1990 Top 10 country hits honored that evening. In addition, *Radio & Records*, a leading music industry trade publication, added another

THE NEW BREED: THE 1980s AND 1990s

147

Although quiet and soft-spoken during interviews, Jackson is a dynamic presence on stage. In addition to his performance skills, he's proved himself a talented songwriter.

Jackson never considered a career in music, because in Newnan — as in many small towns — it was expected that he'd do what everybody else did: go to school, get married, and have a few kids. A music career was simply not part of the picture.

Since his rise to country stardom, Jackson's greatest thrill may be his association with the legendary George Jones. On the liner notes of his debut album, Jackson referred to one of Jones's biggest hits, "Who's Gonna Fill Their Shoes", and said, "I don't know whether I can fill 'em, but I'd sure like to try 'em on." Since Jackson has become acquainted with Jones, the two have formed a mutual admiration society. Jackson's pickup truck sports a bumper sticker reading "I Love George Jones." Jones has a matching pickup, same make and model, with a bumper sticker that says, "I Love Alan Jackson."

accolade when it named Jackson the best new artist of the year.

All eyes and ears were on Jackson's second Arista album, *Don't Rock the Jukebox*, which was released in May 1991. Buyer response was excellent, and the album went platinum.

Working within the solid country parameters that helped establish him as one of country music's more traditional young talents, Jackson broadened his scope both emotionally and musically on his second album. He conveyed the up-tempo side of romance with "Love's Got a Hold on You," but also included such moving ballads as "Someday" and "From a Distance." Jackson also indulged in the country musician's inclination to explore his roots and honor his influences. "Just Playin'

Possum" featured an aural cameo by George Jones, who had also made a guest appearance in Jackson's "Don't Rock the Jukebox" video. "Walkin' the Floor Over Me" brought a new spin to the country standard by Ernest Tubb. Finally, Jackson offered a haunting meditation on Hank Williams called "Midnight In Montgomery."

Jackson admits that singing country music was not something he fantasized about as a kid growing up in Georgia.

The youngest of five children, his family's sense of well-being was drawn from traditional values rather than material wealth.

He started singing as a teenager, performing duets with a friend. They eventually put a band together and played on weekends.

ALAN JACKSON
Born: October 17, 1958; Newnan, Georgia

First hit: "Blue Blooded Woman" (1989)

Other notable hits: "Here in the Real World" (1990), "Chasin' That Neon Rainbow" (1990), "Don't Rock the Jukebox" (1991), "Dallas" (1992)

Awards and achievements: Grand Ole Opry (1991); Academy of Country Music (ACM), Best New Male Vocalist (1991); TNN/*Music City News* Star of Tomorrow (1991); ACM Best Single, Best Album (1992)

Opposite: Jackson's debut album, Here in the Real World, *produced four consecutive number-one singles, and established him as a major country-music star.*

PATTY LOVELESS

Crystal-clear vocals are a Patty Loveless trademark, whether she's singing a heart-tugging ballad such as "Don't Toss Us Away" or a raucous, uptempo scorcher like "I'm That Kind of Girl."

The story of Patty Loveless is actually two stories. The first concerns a 14-year-old girl named Patty Ramey, the daughter of a Kentucky coal miner, who travels to Nashville in 1972, is befriended by Porter Wagoner and Dolly Parton, and becomes the opening act for the Wilburn Brothers. But at 18 she marries the group's drummer, Terry Lovelace, and settles in King's Mountain, North Carolina, where she spends a decade performing at hotels, fairs, and honky-tonks.

The second part of the story skips ahead to Nashville in 1985, when a newly divorced Patty Lovelace impresses MCA Records executive Tony Brown with a five-song demo tape she has financed with her brother. Brown signs her to the label and suggests she change her name; Patty Ramey Lovelace becomes Patty Loveless.

Loveless has notched hit records since 1987, and her *Honky Tonk Angel* album went gold in 1991.

She has been nominated three consecutive times by the Country Music Association as female vocalist of the year. The supple, unrestrained voice that picked up its seasoning during the singer's time in North Carolina has helped Loveless forge a personal style that blends country rock, traditional honky-tonk, and heart-stirring balladry. Her hits include "Hurt Me Bad (In a Real Good Way)," "I'm That Kind of Girl," "Timber (I'm Falling in Love)," "Don't Toss Us Away," and "If My Heart Had Windows."

Loveless's strong voice is balanced by a shy, almost awkward stage presence that pulls an audience toward her. Even after two decades of performing, she doesn't rely on the kind of confident stage professionalism that can seem insincere and overly slick. Loveless appears comfortable only when she's singing, and she pours herself into her songs with genuine conviction. Interestingly, Loveless

had lost track of the progress of country music after leaving Nashville for North Carolina. For years, she couldn't sing country music because club owners and audiences didn't want it. Then, suddenly, she started hearing requests for songs she'd never heard. "Mama He's Crazy," crowds would yell out, but Loveless was unfamiliar with the Judds. "How Blue," yelled others, but the singer hadn't heard of Reba McEntire. To investigate, she bought a few country cassettes and learned that Nashville had rediscovered the kind of music she had favored all her life.

Like Reba McEntire and Kathy Mattea before her, Loveless's climb up the ladder of success was slow, steady, and filled with enough personal growth and memorable music to gain her membership in the Grand Ole Opry.

PATTY LOVELESS

Real name: Patty Ramey Lovelace

Born: January 4, 1957; Pikeville, Kentucky

First hit: "After All" (1987)

Other notable hits: "Timber (I'm Falling in Love)" (1989), "Don't Toss Us Away" (1989), "Chains" (1990), "I'm That Kind of Girl" (1991), "Hurt Me Bad (In a Real Good Way)" (1991), "Jealous Bone" (1992)

Awards and achievements: *Music City News* Star of Tomorrow (1989); TNN/*Music City News* Female Artist (1990); Grand Ole Opry member (1988)

Opposite: *Although Loveless beat the odds by becoming a professional singer while still in her teens, subsequent events slowed her career. Today, she brings a contemporary edge to traditional country music.*

LORRIE MORGAN

The urge to be onstage is among Lorrie Morgan's earliest memories. The youngest child of Anna and George Morgan (a member of the Grand Ole Opry and best known for his hit "Candy Kisses"), Morgan staged "shows" for her family when she was just a child.

Having the great George Morgan as a father opened a few doors, including the one that led to the Opry, where Morgan performed in 1973, at the age of 13. Following her father's death in 1975, she toured with his band and continued to make regular appearances on the Opry. Music became the focal point of her life, and she performed in her share of rough roadhouses and honky-tonks. Later, she joined the Opryland USA theme park and did a two-year tour stint as opening act for George Jones.

A recording contract with MCA ended when Morgan refused to quit the Grand Ole Opry, which she had joined in 1984. In order to support a daughter from an unsuccessful marriage earlier in her career, Morgan sang in clubs, on demo records, and at the Opry. She met singer Keith Whitley when he was cutting a demo of "Does Fort Worth Ever Cross Your Mind." They married in November of 1986 and became parents of a son, Jesse, in June of 1987.

The following year, still confident she could continue her musical career, Morgan signed with RCA Records. Teaming with producer Barry Beckett, Morgan found a combination of songs that showcased her vocal versatility. "Trainwreck of Emotion," her first RCA single, revealed her melancholy country style and became an instant hit.

She was celebrating the release of her first album, *Leave the Light On,* when Whitley, who battled alcohol dependency much of his adult life, died from alcohol poisoning on May 9, 1989. Five months to the day after his death, Morgan accepted a Country Music Association Award for single of the year on Whitley's behalf for "I'm No Stranger to the Rain."

Now with two children depending on her, Morgan resumed a full tour schedule and scored her first Top 10 hit, "Dear Me." Other hits followed: "Out of Your Shoes," "He Talks to Me," "Five Minutes," and "'Til a Tear Becomes a Rose," a studio-engineered duet with her late husband.

Her second album, *Something in Red,* was released in 1991 and included the hit title cut, "We Both Walk," and "A Picture of Me (Without You)." Morgan was also remarried in 1991, to Brad Thompson, the onetime driver for Clint Black's tour bus.

LORRIE MORGAN

Born: June 27, 1959; Nashville, Tennessee

Real name: Loretta Lynn Morgan

First hit: "Trainwreck of Emotion" (1989)

Other notable hits: "Dear Me" (1989), "Out of Your Shoes" (1989), "Five Minutes" (1989), "'Til a Tear Becomes a Rose" (with Keith Whitley, 1990), "Except for Monday" (1991), "We Both Walk" (1991), "A Picture of Me (Without You)" (1991)

Awards and achievements: Grand Ole Opry member (1984); two gold albums; Country Music Association (CMA) Vocal Event of the Year (with Keith Whitley, 1990)

THE NEW BREED: THE 1980s AND 1990s

153

TANYA TUCKER

In 1972, Tanya Tucker came roaring into county music like a Texas tornado with her first single, "Delta Dawn." Fans enjoyed her lusty vocals but were shocked to discover that the husky, sensual voice belonged to a 13-year-old girl.

Born in Seminole, Texas, Tucker was encouraged as a young child to pursue her dream by her parents, Juanita and Beau (who now serves as her manager). After the family relocated to Henderson, Nevada (near Las Vegas), a demo tape financed by Beau Tucker convinced Columbia Records producer Billy Sherrill to sign the teenage singer.

Tucker's first hit, "Delta Dawn," was followed by "Jamestown Ferry," "What's Your Mama's Name," "Blood Red & Goin' Down," and others. By the time she reached her 16th birthday, Tucker had become a sophisticated and successful performer with a string of Top 10 albums: *Delta Dawn, What's Your Mama's Name, Would You Lay with Me (In a Field of Stone), Tanya Tucker,* and *Lovin' and Learnin'*.

Tucker moved to Los Angeles in 1978 and promoted herself as a sex siren via provocative outfits and her *TNT* album, which pushed her style toward rock 'n' roll. Although the album, which featured the hit "Texas (When I Die)," was another best-seller, the move backfired. Her career slowly fizzled, a well-publicized romance with Glen Campbell went bust, and by 1982 Tucker was broke. Backtracking from her pop-rock image, she released two Top 10 country singles, "Pecos Promenade" and "Can I See You Tonight."

Besides her obvious talent and energy, Tucker has a knack for controversy that has shadowed her life and career. Lately she has adopted a rather traditional look . . .

Following a three-year break from recording, Tucker signed with Capitol Records in 1986. Her first Capitol album, *Girls Like Me,* marked a return to the same distinctive, melodic vocals that had made her a star 14 years earlier. She ended her dry spell on the charts with "One Love at a Time," "I'll Come Back as Another

THE NEW BREED: THE 1980s AND 1990s

154

Woman," and "Just Another Love." Tucker reclaimed her position as one of country's leading ladies with her 1987 album, *Love Me Like You Used To*. Several successful singles from the album, including "I Won't Take Less Than Your Love," "If It Don't Come Easy," and the title tune, resulted in two Country Music Association nominations in 1988.

A 1988 battle with alcohol and cocaine addictions was followed a year later by the birth of a daughter, Presley Tanita. After the release of the softer, uncluttered *Strong Enough to Bend*, Tucker delivered a *Greatest Hits* album.

With her 1991 album, *What Do I Do with Me*, Tucker seemed firmly established as one of Music City's most dependable hitmakers. In October of that year the singer gave birth to a son, Beau Grayson, just hours before being named CMA's female vocalist of the year.

... but early in her career Tucker cultivated a powerful sex appeal. Either way, she's an exciting performer who has persevered in the face of financial trouble, rocky romances, and cocaine and alcohol addictions.

TANYA TUCKER

Born: October 10, 1958; Seminole, Texas

First hit: "Delta Dawn" (1972)

Other notable hits: "Would You Lay with Me (In a Field of Stone)" (1974), "The Man That Turned My Mama On" (1974), "San Antonio Stroll" (1979), "Can I See You Tonight" (1981), "One Love at a Time" (1986), "Love Me Like You Used To" (1987), "Strong Enough to Bend" (1988), "Down to My Last Teardrop" (1991)

Awards and achievements: Academy of Country Music Top Ten Female Vocalist (1972); *Music City News* Most Promising Female (1973); Country Music Association Female Vocalist of the Year (1991)

Left and opposite: *Following six years of anonymity on the Houston club circuit, Clint Black vaulted to prominence in 1989 with his debut single, "A Better Man." Although born in New Jersey, Black was brought up in Texas and paid his dues on the Houston club circuit. He brings the essence of traditional Texas honky-tonk to his music.*

P ut Yourself in My Shoes"— that was the song Clint Black was singing in October of 1990. When his debut single, "A Better Man," exploded onto the country charts in May 1989, Clint Patrick Black stepped into a world where frenzied fans will stop at nothing to get a glimpse of their idols, or pick up a prized autograph.

The youngest of four sons born to G. A. and Ann Black, country boy Clint was actually born in Long Branch, New Jersey, where his father was working on a pipeline. But his accent and cowboy hat are the result of being raised in Texas, the place he considers home. When Black was a teenager, his parents recognized his musical abilities and encouraged him to cultivate his

talents. He took their advice and was playing guitar, bass, and harmonica by the time he was 15. Except for brief stints as an ironworker, bait cutter, and fishing guide, he has spent most of his life performing.

With the help of a family friend, Black landed a gig at Houston's Benton Springs club in 1981. Armed with his acoustic guitar, he lived a hand-to-mouth existence on the rowdy Houston club circuit for the next six years, performing a mix of original tunes and traditional songs. During one of those engagements, he met songwriter Hayden Nicholas, who became a frequent collaborator. Later, through the efforts of local promotion man Sammy Alfano, a demo tape that Black and Nicholas had

put together in Nicholas's garage made its way into the hands of Bill Ham, manager of the rock band ZZ Top. Ham loved country music and was looking for a country artist to manage. Struck by the honesty of the lyrics and Black's distinctive vocals, Ham found just what he'd been looking for.

Shortly after hooking up with Ham, Black met Joe Galante, then head of RCA Records' Nashville division. Clint had strolled into his office in Music City and played four demos. Impressed with the confident young singer, Galante agreed to fly to Houston to see him perform. The trip to Houston paid off for both parties because Galante signed Black to an eight-album contract.

When the video of his first single, "A Better Man," was released in May 1989, Black became an instant hit. The single went to number one on the country charts, and Black was suddenly country music's newest sex symbol.

By the time Black's debut album, *Killin' Time*, was released, fans were clamoring for more of his authentic-sounding country songs in traditional honky-tonk arrangements. He obliged with the title cut off the album, which became his second number-one single.

With just two singles, two videos, and one album to his

Industry awards and accolades have come thick and fast for Black, who seems unruffled by it all, perhaps because he was well prepared for his success. From the time of his debut single he willingly met with radio-station reps, pressed the flesh with record retailers—whatever it took to ensure that he would not be just another one-hit wonder. Yet despite the careful career plan, he seems most intent upon doing honest, tradition-based music, and giving his fans the full measure of his talent.

third number-one record in a row. *Billboard* and *Radio & Records* named "A Better Man" and "Killin' Time" the top two country singles of 1989.

As *Killin' Time* went platinum, Black added an American Music Award for new artist of the year to his trophy collection. He also earned two Grammy nominations, one for best vocal performance by a country male and the other for best country song ("A Better Man"), a nomination he shared with cowriter Hayden Nicholas.

The young Texan was also honored at the Academy of Country Music Awards that year. Outfitted in his trademark black Stetson hat, blue jeans, and a tuxedo jacket, Black picked up four awards: He was named the year's top male vocalist and best new male vocalist; *Killin' Time* was named album of the year; and the album's title cut won as single of the year.

Capping off his year of awards, chart-busting records, and industry accolades, Black released two more consecutive number-one singles, "Walkin' Away" and "Nothing's News." According to *Radio & Records*, the singer was the first artist to achieve five number-one records from a debut album in any music format.

Black charted another course of awards and acclaim with the release of "Put Yourself in My Shoes," the title single from his second album. On October 9, 1990, he won the CMA Award for male vocalist of the year. He was also the first recipient of the Nashville Songwriters Association International Songwriter/Artist of the Year award. The album *Put Yourself in My Shoes* was received

credit, Black was honored with three Country Music Association Award nominations in October 1989 and won the Horizon Award, which is bestowed on the performer who has achieved the most in terms of his career.

Late in 1989, Black introduced his next single, "Nobody's Home," on *The Tonight Show*. By early 1990, that tune had become Black's

just as enthusiastically as its predecessor. Released in November of 1990, it was certified platinum that same month.

With his newfound clout, Clint decided to record a tune with the legendary King of the Cowboys, Roy Rogers. The pair teamed up for a video to accompany their "Hold on Pardner" duet, which they performed at the 1991 CMA Awards.

Black's October 1991 marriage to television actress Lisa Hartman fanned the flame of media coverage. The singer seems destined for a long career in country music. He's serious about music and thinks of his writing and performing as his profession. "I don't look on this as a party," he told the *Boston Globe.* That's where [other performers] made their mistake."

Above: *During the 1991 Country Music Association Awards, Black shared the stage with Roy Rogers, the ageless King of the Cowboys.* Below: *Black made headlines in October 1991, when he married television actress Lisa Hartman. The couple exchanged vows in a simple, private ceremony at Black's farm outside Houston.*

CLINT BLACK

Born: February 4, 1962; Long Branch, New Jersey

First hit: "A Better Man" (1989)

Other notable hits: "Killin' Time" (1989), "Nobody's Home" (1989), "Nothing's News" (1990), "Walkin' Away" (1990), "Put Yourself in My Shoes" (1990), "Hold On Pardner" (with Roy Rogers, 1991)

Awards and achievements: Grand Ole Opry member (1991); Country Music Association (CMA) Horizon Award (1989); Academy of Country Music (ACM) Top New Male Vocalist (1989); ACM Top Male Vocalist (1989); CMA Male Vocalist (1990); TNN/*Music City News* Star of Tomorrow (1990)

K. T. OSLIN

Mature and sophisticated, singer-songwriter K. T. Oslin is one of the most outspoken performers in country music.

The rise of K.T. Oslin to the top of the country charts was unusual because it came when she was in her mid-forties, a time in life when many singers begin to fade from view. For Oslin, it represented the beginning of a new career.

Born May 15, 1944, in Crossitt, Arkansas, Kay Toinette Oslin grew up in Mobile, Alabama, and Houston, Texas. As a teen, she discovered rock 'n' roll and the Texas folk music scene, and as a young woman did chorus work in Broadway musicals and jingles for television commercials.

She later became interested in songwriting, and by 1981 her efforts had attracted the attention of Elektra Records, which kept her under contract only briefly.

Oslin fared better at RCA. Her first album, *80's Ladies*, debuted at number 15 on the *Billboard* country album chart and later went gold. In December 1987, Oslin scored her first number-one record with "Do Ya." The following February, she won a Grammy for best female country vocal performance. In April, she was named top new female vocalist by the Academy of Country Music.

Between awards and accolades, Oslin — called "the Diva" by some Nashville industry people — found time to record "Face to Face," a number-one duet with Alabama's Randy Owen. By October of 1988, Oslin was riding the crest of her initial wave of success when she was named female vocalist of the year by the Country Music Association. She became the first female songwriter to win CMA's song of the year award, for the single "80's Ladies."

To make the most of the publicity and media attention lavished on Oslin because of her success, RCA released her second album, *This Woman*, in August of

Oslin's experiences in different facets of show business have given her a perspective that may be unmatched by most other country-music performers.

1988. This highly successful follow-up garnered the singer two more Grammys, including one for her performance of "Hold Me," the chart-topping hit from the album. "Hold Me," which she wrote, also won a Grammy as best country song.

Her third album, 1990's *Love in a Small Town,* was spare and lean and showcased Oslin's songwriting talents by focusing on earthy, slice-of-life vignettes and stories about common folk. Success in videos and as a television actress increased her popularity.

With her sophisticated wit and maturity, Oslin has brought a much-needed female perspective to country music. She once admitted that, as a child, she disliked country music because of its predominantly male point of view. By the early '90s, she was making music to suit herself.

K. T. OSLIN

Real name: Kay Toinette Oslin

Born: May 15, 1944; Crossitt, Arkansas

First hit: "80's Ladies" (1987)

Other notable hits: "Do Ya" (1987), "I'll Always Come Back" (1988), "Hold Me" (1988), "Hey Bobby" (1989), "Come Next Monday" (1990), "Mary and Willie (1991)

Awards and achievements: Grammy Award, Best Country Vocal Performance, Female (1987, 1988); Academy of Country Music (ACM) Top New Female Vocalist (1987); ACM Female Vocalist (1988); Grammy Award, Best Country Song (1988)

From the start of her country-music career, Oslin positioned herself as an innovator who makes clever use of film and video.

THE NEW BREED: THE 1980s AND 1990s

Doug Stone's musical memories go back as far as he can remember. A family snapshot captures three-year-old Doug sitting entranced in front of a record player. At age seven, his mother took him to a Loretta Lynn concert, and the youngster ended up making his stage debut that night at Lynn's invitation.

Stone, whose real name is Doug Brooks, was born in Georgia on June 19, 1956. His parents, Jack Brooks and Gail Menscer, divorced when Stone was 12. At age 16, Stone quit school, bought a mobile home with the money he'd earned performing, and built a portable recording studio. Thus began a journey that included more than a decade of performing in hotel lounges and late-night honky-tonks in the Atlanta area. By the mid-1980s, he had tired of the nightly grind and returned to Newnan, Georgia, where his father owned a diesel-truck repair shop.

Stone went to work as a diesel mechanic. He limited his music performances to weekends at the local VFW lodge, where an aspiring manager named Phyllis Bennett spotted him one night. She introduced herself and told Stone she might be able to promote his career. Stone went along with the idea, and Bennett's efforts eventually led the singer to Epic Records executive Bob Montgomery, who offered Stone an extended recording contract.

Because Garth Brooks had just released his debut album at the

Left: *By the time Doug Stone recorded his second album,* I Thought It Was You, *Sony Records had decided to promote him as a ballad singer with sex appeal.*

time Stone signed with Epic, label executives convinced their new singer to drop his "Brooks" surname. At the time, Doug was writing a song titled "Heart of Stone," and the tune provided him with his stage name.

Epic introduced Stone in the spring of 1990, with the mournful ballad "I'd Be Better Off (In a Pine Box)," the first of several Top Five country hits Stone put together in 1990 and 1991. Others included "Fourteen Minutes Old," "I Thought It Was You," and "A Jukebox with a Country Song." His first album, *Doug Stone*, has sold more than 500,000 copies, and his debut hit, "I'd Be Better Off," earned him a Grammy Award nomination in 1991.

Despite the melancholy nature of many of Stone's best-known songs, the Georgian is a personable, witty ball of energy offstage. He talks with a thick Southern drawl, and he'll openly admit he's survived some mistakes over the years. Today, Stone lives with his third wife, Keri, and two of his four children on a ranch in Newnan, Georgia.

DOUG STONE
Real name: Douglas Brooks
Born: June 19, 1956; Newnan Georgia
First hit: "I'd Be Better Off (In a Pine Box)" (1990)
Other notable hits: "A Jukebox with a Country Song" (1992), "Fourteen Minutes Old" (1990), "In a Different Light" (1991), "I Thought It Was You" (1991), "These Lips Don't Know How to Say Goodbye" (1991)
Awards and achievements: Country Music Association Horizon Award nominee (1991)

Stone seems most comfortable with rousing honky-tonk numbers, perhaps because of the long apprenticeship he served in Atlanta-area lounges and honky-tonks. Still, his melancholy ballads have struck a chord with many listeners, making Stone a potent force on country-music charts.

JOE DIFFIE

Neo-traditionalist Joe Diffie launched a singing career in 1991 that took off with the force of a bottle rocket. His debut single, "Home," was the first record ever to take the number-one position on all three national country charts (*Billboard, Radio & Records*, and the *Bill Gavin Report*) in the same week. It was also the first song to hold that position for two consecutive weeks in both *Gavin* and *R&R*. In addition, Diffie became the first country artist in the history of Epic Records to hit the top of the charts with a debut single.

"Home" may have been the first milestone in Diffie's career, but it was quickly followed by three other singles that hit number one — "If the Devil Danced (In Empty Pockets)," "If You Want Me To," and "New Way to Light Up an Old Flame," all from Diffie's debut album, *A Thousand Winding Roads*.

Despite the heady burst of early success, Diffie had paid his dues for nine years. Back in his home-town of Duncan, Oklahoma, he used to spend his days working at a foundry and his nights playing local clubs. When the foundry closed and his marriage failed, he decided it was time to move to Nashville.

Arriving in Music City in December 1986, Diffie found work at the Gibson Guitar factory, where he stayed for a little over a year. Fortunately for him, his next door neighbor was Johnny Neal of the Allman Brothers Band. Neal helped the hopeful singer secure a writing contract with Forest Hills Music.

Once established as a staff writer, Diffie began singing on

Above and opposite: *Joe Diffie has made a point to cultivate a voice and manner that recall the essence of much of the great country music of the past. Healthy record sales reflect the honesty of his sound.*

demo records. A dead end for some aspiring singers, it worked out well for Diffie. He quickly became one of the most sought-after demo singers in town. Almost every music publisher in Nashville wanted to use Diffie's voice to sell their songs. For example, Diffie's was the voice that Ricky Van Shelton heard when "I've Cried My Last Tear for You" was pitched to him.

One of his demo tapes eventually landed Diffie a recording contract. Publisher Johnny Slate had been pitching "New Way to Fly," which was written by Garth Brooks and Ken Williams, with a demo recorded by Diffie. Slate was trying to interest Bob Montgomery, then head of Artists & Repertoire at Epic Records, in the song. Instead, Montgomery was greatly interested in signing Diffie, even though he didn't have an open slot on his roster. Despite having offers from other labels, Diffie promised to wait until Epic was ready for him. The singer was true to his word and launched his career with Epic a year later.

> **JOE DIFFIE**
> **Born:** December 28, 1960; Tulsa, Oklahoma
> **First hit:** "Home" (1991)
> **Other notable hits:** "If You Want Me To" (1991), "If the Devil Danced (In Empty Pockets)" (1991), "Is It Cold in Here" (1992)
> **Awards and achievements:** First artist in the history of Epic Records to have first single reach the number one position on the charts

THE NEW BREED: THE 1980s AND 1990s

165

RANDY TRAVIS

A voice like his only comes along once in a generation." That's what Minnie Pearl had to say about Randy Travis, who turned the country music world around in 1986, the year he became Nashville's biggest overnight sensation in history. *Storms of Life*, his debut album on Warner Bros. Records, ranks as the first debut album by a country music artist to sell more than a million copies within a year of its release.

It's important to note that Travis's success came when country music sales were at a low point after decreasing steadily for several years. Ricky Skaggs, George Strait, and the Judds had already sent ripples of optimism through the industry by swimming against the flow of pop-influenced, cosmopolitan country music coming out of Nashville in the early 1980s. The meteoric success of Travis turned the tide completely, opening the gates for the flood of successful traditional artists that followed.

Like most "overnight" sensations, Travis spent several hard-working years paying his dues before getting his big break. The second of six children, he was born Randy Traywick on May 4, 1959, in a small North Carolina town, Marshville, located about 30 miles from Charlotte in an area known as the Piedmont Crescent. His father, Harold Traywick, bred horses, raised turkeys, and managed a small construction firm. His mother, Bobbie Traywick, worked in a fabric mill sorting potholders.

Travis diligently started to learn chords on an acoustic guitar at age eight and was singing in a country harmony act called the Traywick

Above and opposite: *Randy Travis cast the mold for the new kind of country music star that has emerged since the late 1980s. He's handsome, humble, business-minded, and loyal to the roots of country music. Young fans respond to his sincerity; older listeners appreciate the echoes of Lefty Frizzell and George Jones.*

Brothers two years later. His teen years were marked by drinking, drug use, and trouble with the law. Before a court date to face a charge of breaking and entering, the troubled 17-year-old signed up for a talent contest at Country Music City USA, Charlotte's pre-eminent country music honky-tonk. There he met Lib Hatcher, the club's manager and part owner. She knew Travis had the stuff to be a star, and with his parents' consent, she appealed to the court to put him on probation and in her care. Travis moved in with Hatcher and her husband and took over as vocalist at Country Music City USA. Hatcher dedicated herself so completely to grooming the young

roustabout that her marriage fell apart.

Although a 1978 association with singer-producer Joe Stampley resulted in a handful of Travis cuts being released on an independent label, Paula Records, Hatcher and Travis felt that the young singer's destiny lay in Nashville, and the two of them moved there in 1980.

Hatcher talked her way into a job managing the Nashville Palace, a tourist-oriented music club and restaurant located in a strip of shops directly across from the entrance of the Opryland Hotel. In time, Travis graduated from the club's floor-mopper to its musical headliner. Regardless, reps of every music company in Nashville turned down a chance to sign Randy Travis.

However, Martha Sharp had yet to hear or see the Palace star. The top talent executive at Warner Bros. (which had already turned Travis down), Sharp finally accepted an invitation from Hatcher in 1985. The moment she heard Travis sing, she knew she wanted to sign him to a record contract. She also knew she would have a hard time convincing her superiors to believe in a singer so obviously devoted to traditional country music. In the face of strong corporate doubt, she succeeded.

Sharp introduced Travis to Kyle Lehning, an accomplished engineer who had worked with Ronnie Milsap and was moving into record production. Lehning produced most of *Storms of Life* (two songs were done by Keith Stegall). Before putting out the album, however, Warners wanted to test the reaction of radio listeners. The

Above: *Travis's formal introduction to the guitar came at the age of eight, when he began to take lessons from Kate Mangum in New Salem, North Carolina.*
Opposite: *Since the late '80s Travis has earned more than $10 million annually in concert fees.*

Music Association and the Academy of Country Music. His albums *Old 8 × 10, No Holdin' Back,* and *Heroes and Friends* extended his million-selling streak into the 1990s. In 1991, as if to confirm his stardom and solidify his link to country music's past, Travis starred in an HBO cable-TV special with the legendary George Jones. And in May of that year, the young star married Lib Hatcher in a private ceremony at Maui, Hawaii.

RANDY TRAVIS
Real name: Randy Traywick
Born: May 4, 1959; Marshville, North Carolina
First hit: "1982" (1986)
Other notable hits: "On the Other Hand" (1987), "Always and Forever" (1987), "Forever and Ever, Amen" (1988), "Too Gone, Too Long" (1988), "Heroes and Friends" (1991), "Better Class of Losers" (1992)
Awards and achievements: Academy of Country Music (ACM) top male vocalist (1986, 1987); Country Music Association (CMA) Horizon Award (1986); *Music City News* male artist of the year (1987); CMA vocalist of the year (1987); CMA album of the year (1987); CMA single of the year (1987); Grammy Award, Best Country Vocal Performance, Male (1988, 1989); *Music City News* entertainer of the year (1988, 1989); Peoples Choice Award, best male musical performer (1989); American Music Award favorite male vocalist, country (1990); *Playboy* Music Poll, male vocalist, country (1991); Grand Ole Opry member (1986)

first single, "On the Other Hand," received a disappointing initial reaction, climbing only to number 67 on the country charts. The next song, "1982," fared much better, introducing Travis to the Top 10. Warners, in an unusual move, decided to give "On the Other Hand" another chance. This time the record took Travis to number one, a position he would visit more than a dozen times in the next five years. *Storms of Life,* in addition to its record-setting sales pace, spent 12 weeks at number one.

With his second album, *Always and Forever,* Travis sealed his status as a country superstar. The album spawned four consecutive number-one songs — "Forever and Ever, Amen," "I Won't Need You Anymore," "Too Gone, Too Long," "I Told You So" — and

spent an astounding ten months atop the country album sales chart.

Along the way, Travis became the model for the new breed of male country star: clean-cut, square-jawed, with a pleasing traditionalism about his wardrobe and manner. He's humble, polite, and reverent toward the stars who preceded him. And Travis is a teetotaler who monitors his diet and prefers a gym to a party. He sings with uncontrived sincerity, and his lower register features a warmth and breadth that brings a mournfulness to all of his work.

Travis dominated many of the awards shows in the late 1980s, winning more than 40 honors in his first four years, including a Grammy Award for best country vocal performance by a male and several awards from the Country

Mary-Chapin Carpenter brings a worldly upbringing and a first-class education to her country-music perspective. She blends several musical styles and attracts fans from diverse backgrounds. Her Grammy-winning 1991 hit, "Down at the Twist and Shout," is urgent and earthy, and proved irresistible to record buyers.

In 1987, Mary-Chapin Carpenter decided she needed a tape of her music to sell in the clubs she played in and around Washington, D.C., so she recorded some songs in the low-tech basement studio of her longtime guitarist, John Jennings. The tape reached a CBS Records executive, who offered her a country record deal. With one new song added, the homemade tape became Carpenter's debut album, *Hometown Girl.*

She was far from a conventional country music prospect. Born in Princeton, New Jersey, and raised in Tokyo and Washington, D.C., Carpenter grew up in an upper-middle-class, urban household. Her father was an editor for *Life* magazine. She attended Brown University and earned a degree in American Studies. Her musical tastes leaned toward rock 'n' roll and to such urban folk singers as Judy Collins and Peter, Paul & Mary. The closest things to a country album she heard while growing up were recordings by folk-music legend Woody Guthrie.

Encouraged by her father, she progressed from at-home guitar-strumming to performing her songs during open-mike night at a club down the street from the family home. She continued to perform while in college and eventually became a local D.C. favorite.

Carpenter's commercial break-through came with *State of the Heart,* her second album for Columbia Records. The album proved a better showcase for her warm alto voice and her eclectic, hard-to-classify sound; in press material, she describes herself as "a singer with an acoustic guitar

Carpenter performed "Down at the Twist and Shout" on the Country Music Association Awards program in October 1991. So infectious was her performance that she had audience member George Bush clapping along with her.

fronting a rock 'n' roll band." Whatever she was, country radio took to her — as did listeners of all musical tastes. The hits from *State of the Heart* include the sassy "How Do," the reflective "This Shirt," and a couple of hard-bitten songs about the end of a relationship, "Never Had It So Good" and "Quittin' Time." The album earned her an Academy of Country Music award for top new female artist.

Her success continued with her third disc, *Shooting Straight in the Dark,* which, like the others, was coproduced by Carpenter and John Jennings. This time, the hits ranged from the harsh honesty of "You Win Again" to the exuberant, Grammy-winning "Down at the Twist and Shout," a Cajun dance tune recorded with a Louisiana band named Beausoleil. In this album, Carpenter continued to probe a wide emotional range with personal insight and keenly observed detail, revealing the folk influence on her music. Once again, she garnered critical praise while expanding her ever-growing group of fans.

MARY-CHAPIN CARPENTER
Born: February 21, 1958; Princeton, New Jersey
First hit: "How Do" (1989)
Other notable hits: "Quittin' Time" (1990), "Down at the Twist and Shout" (1991), "Right Now" (1991)
Awards and achievements: Grammy Award, Best Country Female Vocalist (1992); Country Music Association (CMA) Horizon Award nominee (1990, 1991); American Country Music Best New Female Vocalist (1991)

MARTY STUART

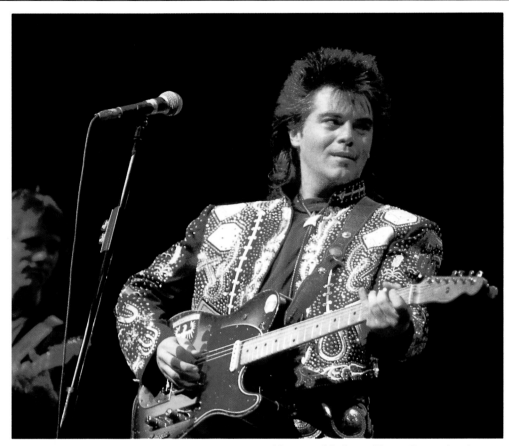

Above and below: *Marty Stuart has been a professional musician since the age of 12, when he toured with a gospel-bluegrass band. Today, he is a colorful performer who owns more than 200 vintage country outfits, as well as a closetful of flashy, custom-made ensembles he calls his "work clothes."*

Although well known for flashy stage attire, Marty Stuart is solidly, seriously grounded in country music. He grew up in Philadelphia, Mississippi, where his father was a factory supervisor and his mother a bank teller. He was hired at age 12 to play mandolin with a gospel-bluegrass band, the Sullivan Family. A year later, he was recruited by the late, legendary Lester Flatt after the singer had split from longtime partner Earl Scruggs. After Flatt's death in 1979, Stuart hooked up with another legend, Johnny Cash, performing with him until 1985.

Along the way, Stuart released two independent albums, *Marty: With a Little Help from His Friends* in 1978 and the acclaimed *Busy Bee Cafe* in 1982. Four years later, he joined CBS Records and put out

Marty Stuart, which featured the Top 20 country hit "Arlene."

In 1989, Stuart emerged on MCA Records with *Hillbilly Rock,* an album that took a fresh perspective on indigenous American music by delving back into the place where the roots of country and rock 'n' roll intertwine. The album's radio hits included the title track, "Western Girls," and a version of Johnny Cash's "Cry, Cry, Cry."

Stuart continued to write prolifically while establishing his own singing career, and his songs were recorded by such diverse performers as Mark Collie, Emmylou Harris, Buck Owens, and Jann Browne.

Stuart's next album, *Tempted,* kept the momentum of *Hillbilly Rock* rolling forward. Like *Hillbilly Rock*, it was produced by Tony Brown and Richard Bennett, and it allowed the singer-instrumentalist to reveal his talent for bluegrass and gospel as well as expanding on his country-rock style. By early 1992, he notched another hit with "The Whiskey Ain't Workin'," a duet he sang with Travis Tritt.

MARTY STUART

Born: September 30, 1958; Philadelphia, Mississippi

First hit: "Hillbilly Rock" (1990)

Other notable hits: Tempted" (1991), "Little Things" (1991), "Till I Found You" (1991), "The Whiskey Ain't Workin'" (with Travis Tritt, 1992)

Awards and achievements: Nominated, TNN/*Music City News* Vocal Collaboration of the Year (1992)

PAM TILLIS

am Tillis, one of country music's hottest newcomers, isn't such a newcomer at all. The daughter of country great Mel Tillis, she appeared with him on the Grand Ole Opry when she was just eight years old. During her career as a performer and songwriter, she moved from one label to another while experimenting with pop, rock, new wave, disco, and jazz before realizing that her roots in country music could not be ignored.

At 16, Tillis was seriously injured in an auto accident. After years of facial surgery and periods at the University of Tennessee and in San Francisco, she earned a living in Nashville as a session singer and songwriter; her songs were recorded by such diverse performers as Juice Newton and Gloria Gaynor. Tillis fronted a Top-40 r&b band for a while, went to England, and eventually landed a record deal. Her first single, "Every Home Should Have One," had a disco feel, while her 1983 album, *Above & Beyond the Doll of Cutey*, was an attempt at new wave.

Resettled in Nashville, she began to score as a country songwriter, and in 1990 she finally claimed her place as a country performer with the release of her Arista album, *Put Yourself in My Place*. The first single from that album, "Don't Tell Me What to Do," hit number one on the charts, and Tillis was nominated for the Country Music Association's Horizon Award in 1991.

Previously married and the mother of a son, Tillis wed songwriter and musical collaborator Bob DiPiero on Valentine's Day in 1991.

PAM TILLIS

Born: July 24, 1957; Plant City, Florida

First hit: "Don't Tell Me What to Do" (1991)

Other notable hits: "Put Yourself in My Place" (1991), "One of Those Things" (1991), "Maybe It Was Memphis" (1992)

Awards and achievements: Nominated for two Country Music Association (CMA) awards (1991)

Pam Tillis, daughter of veteran country star Mel Tillis, has been a successful songwriter in a variety of musical genres—even disco. As a performer, she has been equally diverse, moving from label to label while working in pop, rock, jazz, and other musical styles. For all of that, she has enjoyed her greatest singing and songwriting success in country music. Tillis confirmed her stardom with an enthusiastic performance of "Put Yourself in My Place" at the 1991 Country Music Association Awards show (above).

ROSANNE CASH

Left and opposite: *By scrupulously avoiding formulaic approaches to singing and songwriting, Rosanne Cash has helped to broaden the definition of country music. Her father is country-music legend Johnny Cash.*

Rosanne Cash may belong to one of country music's most famous families, but she came to country music stardom through a side door. She recorded her first album in Germany, her second in Los Angeles. Her hair has changed over the years from inky black to eggplant to light brown and back to natural black. She was openly critical of the old Nashville recording system and has never paid attention to the formulas adhered to by nearly all country hit-makers, big and small.

She also was the only woman to have a number-one country album through the early and mid-1980s, reaching the top spot with *Seven Year Ache* in 1981 and *Rhythm and Romance* in 1985. Her first number-one country song, "Seven Year Ache," also reached number 22 on the pop radio charts. Since then, she has topped the country charts 11 times.

Cash was born in Memphis on May 24, 1955, just days before her father, Johnny Cash, recorded his first songs at Sun Studios. At age 11, she moved with her father and mother, Vivian Liberto, to Ventura, California. Her father divorced Vivian, his first wife, shortly afterward. Although Rosanne remained with her mother in California, she maintained a close relationship with her father.

After high school, Cash joined her father's road show, first as a wardrobe assistant and later as a backup singer. She left the band to live in England for a year, then returned to study drama at Vanderbilt University in Nashville and the Lee Strasberg Institute in Los Angeles.

In 1978, she met singer Rodney Crowell, a singer-songwriter who had just released his solo debut album, *Ain't Living Long Like This*. Crowell helped her produce some songs, which led to her traveling to Germany to record her first album for Ariola Records.

A CBS Records executive heard the album at her father's house and signed her to a recording contract. With Crowell producing, she recorded *Right or Wrong*, which was released in 1979. She and Crowell were married early that year and had their first child, Caitlin, in late 1979. The couple moved to Nashville and recorded *Seven Year Ache* in 1981, further establishing Cash as an effective vocal stylist and revealing her songwriting abilities.

Cash records and tours less frequently than most country performers, devoting time to motherhood (she has three daughters), painting, and writing fiction. Her subsequent albums — *Somewhere in the Stars, Rhythm and Romance, King's Record Shop,* and *Interiors* — often explored her turbulent relationship with Crowell, addressing the ambiguities of modern relationships with honesty, strength, and intimate insight. The couple separated in 1991.

ROSANNE CASH

Born: May 24, 1955; Memphis, Tennessee

First hit: "Couldn't Do Nothin' Right" (1980)

Other notable hits: "Seven Year Ache" (1981), "My Baby Thinks He's a Train" (1981), "I Don't Know Why You Don't Want Me" (1985), "Hold On" (1986), "Tennessee Flat Top Box" (1988), "It's Such a Small World" (with Rodney Crowell, 1988)

Awards and achievements: Grammy Award, Best Country Vocal Performance, Female (1985); Grammy Award, Best Album Package (1988)

Ricky Skaggs is a proficient multi-instrumentalist who has won awards for his musicianship as well as for his vocal work. On stage, he regularly trades off between a fiddle, a mandolin, and acoustic and electric guitars.

Ricky Skaggs served an impressive apprenticeship before getting the opportunity to record his own music for a major record company. He quickly proved he'd learned his lessons well, creating 16 Top 10 hits between 1981 and 1986 with a fresh sound that updated bluegrass and honky-tonk music with breathtaking musical arrangements and a modern rhythmic bounce. The former bluegrass prodigy's success turned country music in a new direction and set the stage for the new stars of recent years and the return to traditional sounds.

Skaggs was born July 18, 1954, in Cordell, Kentucky. By age five, he was taking mandolin lessons from his father and learning traditional mountain songs from his mother. At seven, the youngster performed on a TV show hosted by bluegrass stars Flatt and Scruggs. At age 15, he joined the band headed by one of his idols, Ralph Stanley. In 1972, at age 17, he recorded an album with childhood friend Keith Whitley, also a member of Stanley's band.

Skaggs spent the mid-1970s as a member of several highly acclaimed, progressive bluegrass bands, including the Country Gentlemen, the New South, and his own Boone Creek. Emmylou Harris recruited him to join her Hot Band in the late 1970s, and Skaggs began recording solo albums for an independent label, Sugar Hill Records.

Skaggs's independent recordings set the stage for his first Nashville album for Epic Records. *Waitin' for the Sun to Shine* surprised every country music executive with its huge sales, topping 500,000 in sales within a year and earning Skaggs his first Country Music Association honors. The young singer was named male vocalist of the year and also won the Horizon Award for most significant career growth. His next three albums sold in equally impressive numbers. In 1985 Skaggs was given country music's most prestigious annual honor: He was named entertainer of the year by the Country Music Association. He went on to win Grammy Awards for best country instrumental performance in 1983, 1984, and 1986, and he shared the 1987 vocal duo of the year award with his wife, Sharon White. He also produced Dolly Parton's country music comeback album, *White Limozeen.*

Of his role in revitalizing country music in the 1980s, Skaggs says: "I set out to create a more traditional, back-to-basics kind of sound. [I wanted to] bring forth the mandolin, fiddle, banjo, and steel guitars that had really been lost by the wayside. It was something I felt like the fans wanted, and it was certainly something I wanted."

RICKY SKAGGS
Born: July 18, 1954: Cordell, Kentucky
First hit: "You May See Me Walkin'" (1981)
Other notable hits: "Crying My Heart Out Over You" (1982), "Heartbroke" (1982), "Highway 40 Blues" (1983), "Don't Cheat in Our Hometown" (1984), "Cajun Moon" (1986), "Same Ol' Love" (1992)
Awards and achievements: Grand Ole Opry member (1982); Grammy Award, Best Country Instrumental Peformance (1983, 1984, 1986); Country Music Association (CMA) Horizon Award (1982); CMA Best Male Vocalist (1982); CMA Entertainer of the Year (1985);

Above: *Skaggs is among the few major artists in Nashville who is self-managed.* Below: *Skaggs stoutly resisted the country-pop sound that swept country music in the '80s, and remained true to bluegrass and other traditional sounds.*

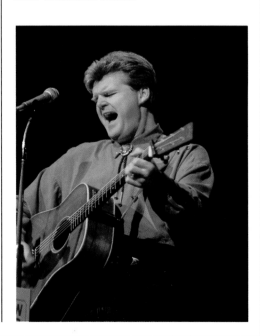

Above: Personal problems and an unwise reliance on his famous father's material in the 1960s suggested that the career of Hank Williams, Jr., might be short-lived. But Williams eventually chose a more moderate lifestyle and found his own voice as a performer. Opposite: *Williams's patriotic fervor is just one expression of his upbeat nature —a mindset that undoubtedly helped him to overcome massive injuries suffered in a near-fatal fall in 1975.*

Hank Williams, Jr., performed his first concert at the tender age of eight. He recorded his first song — and Top 10 hit — at 14. He scored his next hit at age 16. But, as suggested by the title and lyrics of that second hit, "Standin' in the Shadows," the young man who had changed his name from Randall Hank Williams to Hank Williams, Jr., was quite aware that he was riding the coattails of his legendary father. Hank, Sr., died from the effects of hard living in 1953, leaving behind a haunting legacy for his three-year-old son. Hank, Jr., spent the 1960s performing his father's songs, adhering to the career guidance offered by his mother, and indulging a growing appetite for drugs and alcohol.

In 1974, Williams decided to step out of his father's long shadow and stand on his own. Against the wishes of his mother, Audrey, he moved from Nashville to Cullman, Alabama, initiated a divorce from his second wife, and began an album that combined Southern rock, Delta blues, and rebel country.

Williams celebrated the completion of this new, ground-breaking collection of songs by going on a hunting and hiking trip in Montana. During an outing, he suffered massive head injuries when he slipped on a ledge and fell 500 feet down a jagged, rocky slope of Mount Ajax. Over the next eight months, he underwent several operations to reconstruct his face. Adding to the stress of his rehabilitation was the death of his mother three months after his fall.

While the singer recuperated, the landmark *Hank Williams & Friends* album was released. It was a bold departure for Williams and featured contributions from country rock performers such as Charlie Daniels, Toy Caldwell of the Marshall Tucker Band, and Chuck Leavell of the Allman Brothers. The album's rock edges alienated Williams from the Nashville establishment and from his longtime record company, MGM Records. The album included the song "Living Proof," a lament about a drunkard's taunt that Hank, Jr., would never be as good as his father. Williams later adopted it as the title of his 1979 autobiography.

THE NEW BREED: THE 1980s AND 1990s

179

of 10,000 or more fans, a rarity for a country music artist at that time. And, he continued to pull in those numbers for the remainder of the decade. By the end of the 1980s, Williams's total sales topped the $25 million mark.

Despite his success, Williams was shunned by the established country music awards organizations, who viewed him as an outsider who had been openly critical of Nashville's recording and business practices. Eventually, the country music industry began to come around. In 1985, Williams received a video of the year award from the Country Music Association for "All My Rowdy Friends Are Coming over Tonight." When accepting the trophy, he quipped, "You know, I make a little audio, too."

Two years later, Williams began to gain the recognition that seemed

A music-establishment outsider for many years, Williams did not make a lot of friends with comments that were critical of Nashville business and recording practices.

Nashville may have been miffed by the candor of Williams's remarks about Music City, but success is hard to ignore; Nashville had embraced Williams by 1987.

Williams proved how well he had recovered by releasing *The New South* in 1977, a pointed statement about his vision of a new musical style. Produced by Waylon Jennings, *The New South* was Williams's first album since joining Curb/Warner Bros., the new record company established by music industry mogul Mike Curb. The album marked the beginning of an association with the label that would last until 1992.

Williams closed the 1970s by setting personal sales records. He released the *Family Tradition* album in April 1979 and followed it with *Whiskey Bent and Hellbound* in October. Both albums topped 500,000 in sales within a year. Thirty years after his birth on May 26, 1949, in Shreveport, Louisiana, Williams had succeeded in forging his own identity. Manager and close friend Merle Kilgore declared via song that he wasn't going to call Williams "Junior" anymore, which was his way of acknowledging Hank's new, unique style.

By 1982, Williams had attracted a fanatically loyal following. In concert, he regularly drew crowds first Grammy Award for the same father-son vocal duet.

The pervasive influence of Williams's introduction of a rock sound to country music became apparent in the late 1980s with the success of the Kentucky HeadHunters, Travis Tritt, Pirates of the Mississippi, and others. Williams championed the youthful new sound with his hit song "Young Country" in 1988, and he has served as an elder statesman of progressive country music to the newcomers.

In 1990, Williams married Mary Jane Thomas; the marriage was his fourth. The following year, he terminated several long-running business associations when he switched his concert bookings to the William Morris Agency and signed a multiyear recording contract with Capricorn Records.

Williams has come to terms with his father's legacy without forsaking his own identity as a performer.

so long overdue. The Academy of Country Music kicked off his big year by naming him entertainer of the year, and a few months later, the CMA granted him their version of that same honor. The CMA also gave the video of the year award to his video version of "My Name Is Bocephus." In 1988, he was again named entertainer of the year by both country music organizations, and *Born to Boogie* was designated album of the year by the CMA. In 1989, he received the CMA's award for vocal event of the year for his hit "There's a Tear in My Beer," a high-tech duet recording that combined Williams's voice with a newly discovered, long-lost audio track of Hank, Sr. He also won an award for the video rendition of the song, which used special effects to place the younger Williams into old film footage of the senior Williams in performance. In 1990, Hank, Jr., won his

HANK WILLIAMS, JR.
Real name: Randall Hank Williams
Born: May 26, 1949; Shreveport, Louisiana
First hit: "Long Gone Lonesome Blues" (1964)
Other notable hits: "Whiskey Bent And Hell Bound" (1979), "Family Tradition" (1979), "All My Rowdy Friends" (1981), "Hotel Whiskey" (with Clint Black, 1992), "There's a Tear in My Beer" (with Hank Williams, 1990), "Born to Boogie" (1987)
Awards and achievements: Academy of Country Music, Entertainer of the Year (1986, 1987, 1988); Country Music Association (CMA) Entertainer of the Year (1987, 1988); CMA Vocal Collaboration (1989); Grammy Award, Best Country Vocal Collaboration (1990)

When Kix Brooks and Ronnie Dunn exploded onto the country music scene in 1991, the hard-edged honky-tonk music on their debut album, *Brand New Man*, gave the illusion that the pair had been singing together a long time. In reality, they had known each other less than a year when their record was released.

Leon "Kix" Brooks, a high-energy native of Shreveport, Louisiana, grew up near the home of singer Johnny Horton. Although Brooks eventually established himself as one of Nashville's top songwriters, he still dreamed of being a recording artist. He pitched himself as a singer to Tim DuBois, head of Arista Records in Nashville, who kept Brooks's demo tape on file.

Ronnie Dunn's father performed in a country band and gave young Ronnie his first taste of playing professionally. A flirtation with the ministry ended when the normally laid-back Dunn was caught playing in honky-tonks and was kicked out of school. When he arrived in Nashville from Tulsa, Oklahoma, his only claim to fame was having won the nationwide 1990 Marlboro Talent Search. Part of the prize included some studio time with top Nashville producer and engineer Scott Hendricks. Hendricks recorded Dunn and took the material over to Tim DuBois.

DuBois suggested to Brooks and Dunn that they team up, and offered them a recording contract. A chemistry gradually developed between the pair as they started writing, recording, and performing together. Their first single, "Brand New Man," delivered a no-holds-

Above: *The easygoing manner of Ronnie Dunn (left) complements Kix Brooks's more flamboyant style.* Below: *Although Brooks has been a fixture in Nashville for years, Dunn is a relative newcomer to country music. In 1992 the duo was honored by the Academy of Country Music with awards for vocal duet and new vocal group.*

barred honky-tonk sound with a contemporary edge, and it soon hit the top of the country charts. Their follow-up single, "My Next Broken Heart," also went number one; country music now had a new star duo.

BROOKS & DUNN

Real names: Kix Brooks; Ronnie Dunn

Born: (Brooks) May 12, 1955; Shreveport, Louisiana
(Dunn) June 1, 1953; Coleman, Texas

First hit: "Brand New Man" (1991)

Other notable hits: "My Next Broken Heart" (1991), "Neon Moon" (1992)

Awards and achievements: Academy of Country Music Top Vocal Duet, New Vocal Group (1992)

DIAMOND RIO

Named for a trucking company in Harrisburg, Pennsylvania, Diamond Rio is comprised of six world-class musicians. Each brings a different influence to the band, which accounts for its progressive mix of country, rock, and jazz.

Lead singer Marty Roe and lead guitarist Jimmy Olander were both child prodigies who were professional musicians by the age of 12. Roe learned his first song at the tender age of three, and Olander was teaching banjo while still a child. Roe joined Diamond Rio (then called the Tennessee River Boys) in 1984; Olander came aboard after stints with Rodney Crowell and Duane Eddy.

The remaining band members are diverse. Gene Johnson adds mandolin to the band's unique sound. Classically trained pianist Dan Truman is also a top-notch fiddler and acoustic guitar player, and a former member of the Brigham Young University Young Ambassadors. Bass player and vocalist Dana Williams was playing bluegrass music for a living at the age of 12. Finally, drummer Brian Prout brings a rock influence to Diamond Rio.

Arista Records executive Tim DuBois signed the group to a recording contract after seeing them open a show for George Jones. Still known as the Tennessee River Boys at the time, the members adopted their new name soon after.

Diamond Rio's debut single, "Meet in the Middle," went to number one on the country music charts—the first time a debut single by a country vocal group had done so. Their second single, "Mirror, Mirror," climbed to number three.

DIAMOND RIO

Real names: Marty Roe; Dana Williams; Brian Prout; Dan Truman; Gene Johnson; Jimmy Olander

Born: (Roe) December 28, 1960; Lebanon, Ohio

(Williams) May 22, 1961; Dayton, Ohio

(Prout) December 4, 1955; Troy, New York

(Truman) August 29, 1956; St. George, Utah

(Johnson) August 10, 1949; Jamestown, New York

(Olander) August 26, 1961; Minneapolis, Minnesota

First hit: "Meet in the Middle" (1991)

Other notable hits: "Mirror, Mirror" (1991), "Mama Don't Forget To Pray For Me" (1992)

Awards and achievements: Academy of Country Music, Best Vocal Group (1992)

Diamond Rio appeared at their first International Country Music Fan Fair in Nashville in 1991. While there, they met fans who enjoy their tight, contemporary sound.

CARLENE CARTER

Carlene Carter is the daughter of Carl Smith and June Carter, and stepdaughter to Johnny Cash. Her stepsister is Rosanne Cash and British rocker Nick Lowe is one of her ex-husbands. This mixed bag of musical influences has encouraged Carter to work in a variety of styles, and has made her one of country music's more interesting singer-songwriters.

Carlene Carter springs from the most deeply rooted family tree in country music. A granddaughter of the legendary Maybelle Carter, Carlene's parents are June Carter Cash and Carl Smith. Country Music Hall of Fame member Johnny Cash is her stepfather, and Goldie Hill, a popular country singer during the 1950s, is her stepmother. Carter's extended family also includes stepsister Rosanne Cash and former brothers-in-law Marty Stuart and Rodney Crowell.

Considering her heritage, it's no surprise that Carter found herself with a hit country album in 1990 when Warner Bros. Records released *I Fell in Love*. The energetic singer/songwriter garnered recognition and acclaim with the title track, which reached the number-three position on *Billboard*'s country chart.

But before finding success as a country performer, Carter ventured into other types of music. She began defining her own musical style while attending Nashville's Belmont College and landed her first record deal in 1978. Her quest for a sound she could call her own led her from her country roots to pop to rhythm and blues. Eventually, it led her to England. There she was married for a short time to rock 'n' roll singer Nick Lowe. (A bride at 15 and a mother at 16, Carter has been married and divorced three times.)

With five albums under her belt but no hits to her credit, Carter sought success as a songwriter. Such diverse acts as Emmylou Harris ("Easy From Now On"), the Doobie Brothers ("One Step Closer"), and the Go-Go's ("I'm the Only One") recorded her songs. She credits her mother, June Carter Cash, for the motivation to start writing. "Mama told me it was the best way to make a living. I didn't know how to start so I took a Tchaikovsky chord

Although she had a record deal of her own as early as 1978, Carter did not come to the fore as a performer until 1990.

progression and wrote it out, and then I wrote a song to that chord progression with a different melody. That's how I figured out the process," Carter recalls.

In 1990, Carter became Nashville's unofficial homecoming queen when she not only returned to her country roots but also moved back to Music City. Three years earlier, she had joined the Carter Family for a London performance and toured with the group for two years, preparing her for her return to Nashville's music scene. At last, things seemed ready to fall into place. Her varied experiences and explorations of different musical styles inevitably influenced the *I Fell in Love* album. Combining the bluegrass-inspired gospel of the Carter Family with the rockabilly sound of her ex-husband, Nick Lowe, Carter has forged a mature, honest style that is uniquely her own.

CARLENE CARTER

Real name: Rebecca Carlene Smith

Born: September 26, 1955; Madison, Tennessee

First hit: "I Fell in Love" (1990)

Other notable hits: "Come on Back" (1990), "The Sweetest Thing" (1991)

Awards and achievements: Grammy nominee, Best Country Performance, Female (1991)

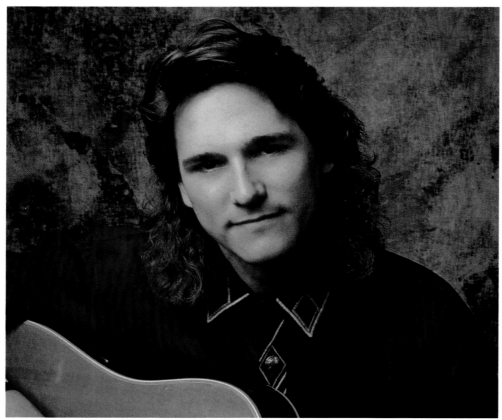

Above: *Billy Dean's good looks contributed to his past success as an actor, but when he was selected as a finalist for the 1991 Country Music Association Horizon Award, it was clear that he had much more going for him than a handsome face.* Opposite: *Dean is more pop-oriented than some of his contemporaries, and favors contemplative songs.*

Although Billy Dean once made his living as an actor in TV commercials, music has always been his first love. He grew up in Quincy, Florida, and began his musical career singing in his father's band. A mechanic by trade, the elder Dean taught his son to play guitar and encouraged him to develop his musical talent. Dean touts his late father as a major musical influence, along with more recognizable names such as Merle Haggard, Jim Reeves, Marty Robbins, and Dean Martin.

Dean attended East Central Junior College in Decatur, Mississippi, on a basketball scholarship. After a brief move to Las Vegas, he returned home in 1982, crossed the state line to Georgia, and entered the regional Wrangler Country Star Search talent contest in Bainbridge. After winning the state final, he advanced to the national contest, held at the Grand Ole Opry in Nashville. Although he didn't win the national prize, he was one of the top ten finalists. More importantly, he decided to settle in Music City.

To support himself, he formed a band and started to tour, opening shows for such name acts as Mel Tillis, Gary Morris, Ronnie Milsap, and Steve Wariner. He began to concentrate on songwriting as well, enjoying a fair degree of success when Milsap, Randy Travis, the Oak Ridge Boys, Les Taylor, the Bama Band, and Shelly West recorded his songs. Eventually his songwriting and singing caught the ear of publisher/producer Jimmy Gilmer, who quickly signed Dean to a songwriting contract in 1988. A record deal with Capitol Nashville/SBK soon followed.

"Only Here for a Little While," Dean's first single and music video from his debut album *Young Man*, showcased the singer's boyish appeal and clear-voiced singing style. The follow-up single, "Somewhere in My Broken Heart", which he cowrote with award-winning songwriter Richard Leigh, showed the more emotional side of Billy Dean to country audiences.

The song hit the top of the country charts and also received airplay on adult contemporary radio stations; it reached the Top 10 on the A/C charts. Dean also received a Grammy nomination for best country performance by a male for this smooth, romantic hit. Dean followed this impressive first album with *Billy Dean*, which showcased his sensitive, personal side on such tunes as "Small Favors" and "You Don't Count the Cost."

BILLY DEAN

Born: April 2, 1962; Quincy, Florida

First hit: "Only Here for a Little While" (1990)

Other notable hits: "Somewhere in My Broken Heart" (1991), "The Wind" (1992)

Awards and achievements: Academy of Country Music, Best New Male Vocalist (1992)

THE NEW BREED: THE 1980s AND 1990s

MIKE REID

A lthough Mike Reid found considerable success as an NFL lineman with the Cincinnati Bengals from 1970 to 1975, he retired from football at age 28 to devote himself to his first passion—music.

Wisely taking full advantage of his sports celebrity to give his musical career a boost, he toured with a couple of bands before striking out as a solo artist. While touring, Reid also concentrated on songwriting.

Reid moved to Nashville in 1980, after a music publisher offered him a songwriter's contract.

Above: *When he was a professional football player in Cincinnati, Mike Reid entertained elementary-school children with private concerts.*

Reid found himself on the fast track two years later, when his song "Inside" was taken to number one by Ronnie Milsap. Reid became firmly established as a hit songwriter, most notably for "Stranger in My House," which garnered him a Grammy Award for best country song in 1984. His tune "Lost in the Fifties Tonight" received Grammy and Country Music Association nominations for song of the year. Prominent artists who have recorded his tunes include Tanya Tucker, Anne Murray, Lee Greenwood, Barbara Mandrell, Joe Cocker, the Judds, Alabama, and Bonnie Raitt.

Reid made his recording debut with "Old Folks," a 1987 duet with Ronnie Milsap. In 1989 Steve Buckingham of Columbia Records approached Reid about a recording contract. The result was his debut album, *Turning for Home*, which spawned Reid's first number-one record as a performer, "Walk on Faith."

Although he has made a successful transition from football to music, Reid is still remembered as a hero of the gridiron. In 1987, he was inducted into the National Football Foundation's College Football Hall of Fame.

Reid has enjoyed considerable success as a songwriter. Bonnie Raitt, who recorded his "I Can't Make You Love Me," is just one of many pop and country stars who have recorded his songs.

MIKE REID

Born: May 24,1947; Altoona, Pennsylvania

First hit: "Walk On Faith" (1991)

Other notable hits: "'Til You Were Gone" (1991), "I'll Stop Loving You" (1991)

Awards and achievements: Grammy Award, Best Country Song (1983, 1985)

MARK CHESNUTT

Mark Chesnutt's first nationally released song, "Too Cold at Home," helped establish the singer as one of the new traditionalists currently changing the look and sound of country music. Although only 26 years old when he was exposed to a national audience for the first time, Chesnutt had already racked up a decade of performing experience.

He was born in Beaumont, Texas, a blue-collar town of factories and oil refineries in East Texas. His father, Bob Chesnutt, was a regional country music performer who spent the late 1950s and early 1960s searching for the big break. The elder Chesnutt finally gave up the hunt in 1970 in order to devote more time to his family. Mark, however, was performing in honky-tonks across Eastern and Central Texas before he was 20 and began recording in Texas in 1982.

"Too Cold at Home" was a success in Chesnutt's home state and led the singer to MCA Records vice president and chief talent scout Tony Brown, who signed him to the label. The *Too Cold at Home* album, produced by Mark Wright, yielded the hit title cut and "Blame It on Texas," "Your Love Is a Miracle," "Brother Jukebox," and "Broken Promise Land." Wright also produced Chesnutt's follow-up album, *Longnecks and Short Stories,* released in March 1992.

Chesnutt's success has fulfilled not only his own dreams, but those of his father: Although Bob Chesnutt died in November 1990 of a massive heart attack, he lived just long enough to see his son's first song climb toward the top of the country music charts.

Mark Chesnutt achieved an astounding five number-one songs from his debut album. His devotion to a traditional sort of country sound has paid handsome dividends.

MARK CHESNUTT

Born: September 6, 1963; Beaumont, Texas

First hit: "Too Cold at Home" (1990)

Other notable hits: "Brother Jukebox" (1991), "Your Love Is a Miracle" (1991), "Blame It on Texas" (1991), "Old Flames Have New Names" (1992)

Awards and achievements: Nominated, Country Music Association Horizon Award (1991)

INDEX

INDEX

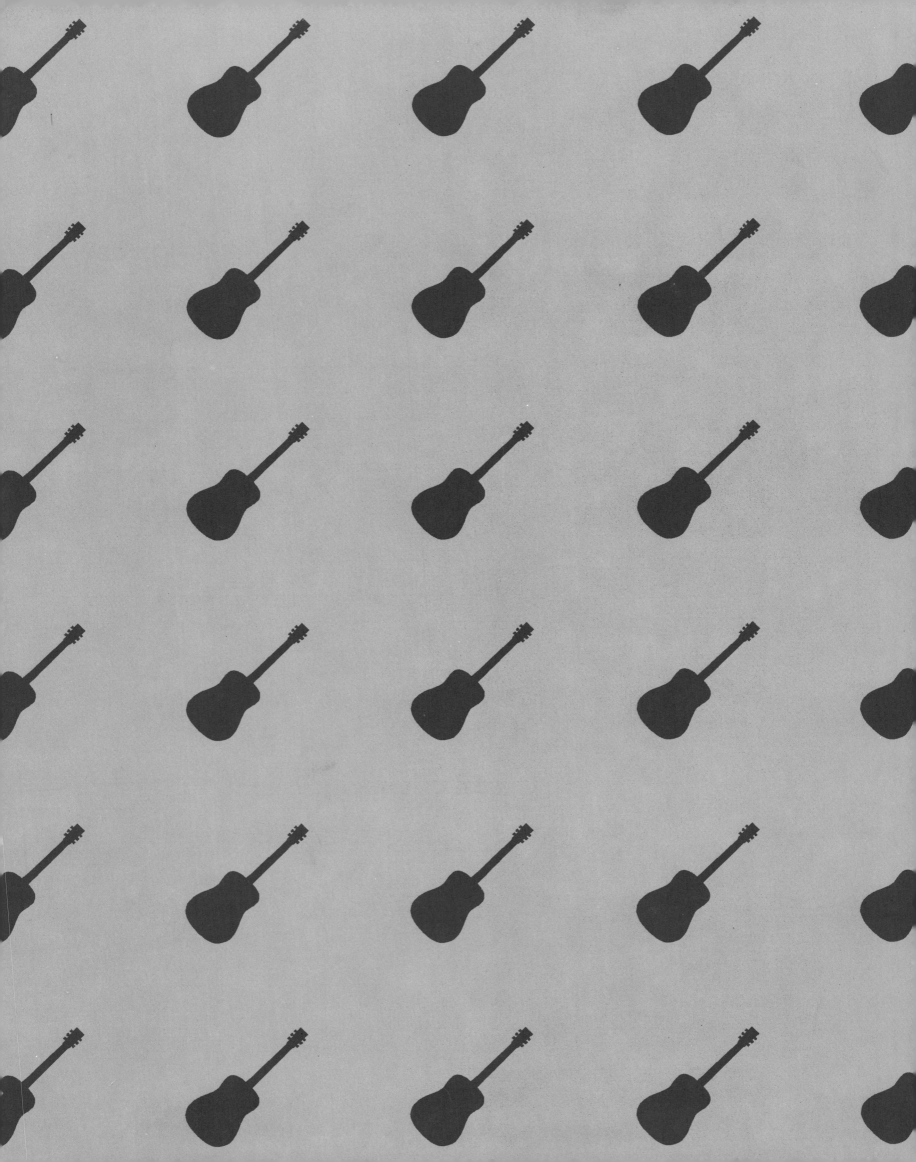